Bunyan hi[...] [...] [...]
strates, adher[...]
tions advocat[...]
Unlike most [...]
teenth centur[...]
indebted to t[...]
for various e[...]
emphases tended to give his own thoug[...]
something of a hybrid character, and in
one way at least this hybrid character was
significant: Luther's influence gave to his
writing and preaching a more personal
appeal that would have been the case had
he relied solely on the more logic-bound
orthodox Calvinism.

John Bunyan presents the life and thought
of a major figure in the Reformation whose
theological influence has too often been
underestimated. Included are such valuable aids to student and scholar as a Glossary, a Bibliography of Bunyan's Works,
a list of selected secondary sources on
Bunyan, and an Index.

COURTENAY STUDIES IN
REFORMATION THEOLOGY

2 JOHN BUNYAN

COURTENAY STUDIES IN
REFORMATION THEOLOGY

2

JOHN BUNYAN

RICHARD L. GREAVES

Assistant Professor of Humanities, Michigan State University

WM. B. EERDMANS PUBLISHING COMPANY
GRAND RAPIDS, MICHIGAN

Set in 11 point Garamond, 1 point leaded
and printed in Great Britain by
Burgess & Son (Abingdon) Limited, Station Road, Abingdon,
Berkshire

Editorial Advisory Board

Sutton Courtenay Publications

Courtenay Library of Reformation Classics

1. The Work of William Tyndale. 446 pages.
   Edited by G. E. Duffield.
2. The Work of Thomas Cranmer. 416 pages.
   Introduced by J. I. Packer.
3. The Work of William Perkins. 650 pages.
   Introduced and edited by I. Breward.
4. The Homilies.
   Introduced by J. E. Tiller.

Courtenay Studies in Reformation Theology

1. John Calvin. 240 pages.
   A symposium edited by G. E. Duffield.
2. John Bunyan. 176 pages.
   R. L. Greaves.

Courtenay Reformation Portraits

1. Thomas Cranmer by Gerlach Flicke.
2. John Calvin after Holbein.

Both in full colour mounted in sturdy folders.

Further publications in preparation: details from the publishers.

Foreword

Geoffrey F. Nuttall

There are some books, which when one sees one exclaims, 'What a good idea! I wonder why no one ever thought of that before!' And this is one of them. Bunyan still exercises a remarkable fascination over men's minds. Pilgrims (in a less biblical sense than he would approve) visit in increasing numbers the Bunyan Museum and Library at Bunyan Meeting, Bedford, as the church to which he ministered has long been known. There are new and attractive biographies, in English, French and German, and numerous articles elucidating particular points in Bunyan's life or discussing literary or bibliographical issues that arise from a study of his writings. *The Pilgrim's Progress* continues to be translated into fresh European, Asian and African languages and dialects, and in England alone sells at about 10,000 copies per annum. *Grace Abounding* can still, I know for a fact, make an unexpected and lasting impact on a reader's life. Both books have appeared in handsome Oxford editions, with discerning prefaces and notes by Professor Sharrock. Plans are afoot for a new collected edition of Bunyan. But we have had no study of his theology.

In the last quarter of a century Puritanism more generally has had a good press. Biographies of Puritans, studies of Puritan politics, economics and sociology abound. Few writers, however, have penetrated at all deeply into Puritan theology. In any case Bunyan does not usually receive attention as a theologian. This is curious. Bunyan was a considerable writer, and many of his

7

books, by no means only those written in a polemic spirit, are profoundly theological. Whatever we may think of it to-day, his thought possesses at once the intellectual satisfaction and the psychological appeal of a theology which was intelligible to a man unversed in the technicalities of the schools and was always kept close to life and life's manifold experience. From this point of view, Bunyan gives us Puritan theology at its most characteristic.

Dr. Greaves' study of Bunyan's theology has extended over several years and has been thorough. He is familiar with the period and its thinking as well as with Bunyan's own writings. He has written a very good book. It breaks new ground. He would not wish it to be called definitive. If he stimulates someone to (say) a closer examination of Bunyan's theology as expressed in the unusual medium of dramatic imagery, no one will be better pleased than he.

New College, London
April 1969

Contents

Preface

Richard L. Greaves

THE HERITAGE of the Puritan-sectarian tradition to Anglo-American civilisation is a significant one. From that tradition have come progressive principles in support of education, liberty, democracy, and social concern. Those principles were thoroughly grounded in the religious convictions of those who comprised this tradition. Indeed, the religious beliefs themselves have been widely embraced by subsequent generations of English Nonconformists, and by the spiritual followers of the Puritans of New England and the pioneering migrants who spread out to settle the American wilderness.

This book is a study of the thought of one of those men—a Bedfordshire tinker with the vision of Paul, the conviction of Luther, and the commitment to freedom of Milton. John Bunyan was not a university graduate, but the fervour of his preaching and the warmth of his personality brought him a wider following than that attained by nearly all of his university-trained contemporaries. His theology cut through the impersonal, scholastic mould commonly imposed on English Calvinism in the seventeenth century, until its core was a living, vibrant awareness of divine grace. The ability to communicate that living awareness to others made Bunyan immensely successful as a preacher to the common man.

In presenting Bunyan's thought, a glossary of technical terms has been included for the benefit of the non-specialist. For the sake of brevity and clarity, citations to Bunyan's myriad works in the footnotes are made by Roman numerals rather than titles. A bibliography of Bunyan's works at the end of the book correlates the titles with the Roman numerals.

The author wishes to express special appreciation to Dr. Geoffrey F. Nuttall for his inspiration and guidance of this work from its inception to its completion. In its original, expanded form it was awarded the degree of Doctor of Philosophy by the University of London. It is also a pleasure to acknowledge the encouragement and assistance of the following scholars: Provost Richard Schlatter of Rutgers University; Dr. Ted Underwood of the University of Minnesota; Dr. Benjamin Carr of Morehead State College; Dr. E. P. Y. Simpson of Massey University, New Zealand; Dr. John New of Brown University, Rhode Island; Dr. Gordon Rupp of Cambridge University; Dr. Roger Sharrock of London University; and Dr. Robert Hannen of Central Theological Seminary. To the staffs of the following libraries I express my appreciation for making available original copies of the works of Bunyan and his contemporaries: the British Museum; the library of New College, London; the Bodleian, Oxford; Dr. Williams' Library, London; Friends House, London; and the William Andrews Clark Memorial Library, University of California at Los Angeles. The congregation of Bunyan Meeting, Bedford, in extending to me the hospitality of their homes and their collection of Bunyan memorabilia, evoked the warmth of the Pilgrim's spirit. Mr. G. E. Duffield has provided valuable editorial assistance. I wish to thank the editors of *Church History* for allowing me to use the substance of Chapter 4, which appeared in their journal in June 1967. Above all, I owe an untold debt of gratitude to my wife, whose personal sacrifices, unfailing encouragement, and clerical assistance made this study possible. In her shines the spirit of Christiana.

Introduction

THE SEVENTEENTH CENTURY, aptly referred to by historians as the century of revolution, was particularly an age of turmoil and change in England. Within that century no two decades witnessed more upheaval and revolutionary manifestations than those of 1640 to 1660. At no other time and in no other place in Europe did the revolutionary ferment so thoroughly grip an entire society. Politically the revolution overthrew first a monarchy, then a republican commonwealth, and finally a military protectorate—only to restore monarchical government. Economically the mercantile philosophy of the commercial revolution as practised by the Commonwealth and Protectorate governments of Oliver Cromwell brought forth the Navigation Act of 1651 and the ensuing war with the Dutch. Intellectually the brilliant mind of Thomas Hobbes called for the restructuring of political institutions on frankly secular grounds, and the revolutionary Copernican hypothesis won increasing acceptance at Oxford University through the work of Seth Ward, the Savilian Professor of Astronomy.

The revolutionary fervour of the decades 1640–1660 was especially conducive to varied expressions of radicalism. In the political realm John Lilburne and the Levellers advocated an extension of the franchise and the promulgation of a written constitution. The religiously-oriented Fifth Monarchy movement called for the political rule of the saints preparatory to the millennial advent of the Messiah. Some, such as John Rogers and Thomas Venner, went so far as to demand the use of force, if necessary, in order for the saints to obtain the desired political power. Economic radicalism was manifested in the Digger movement of Gerrard Winstanley, who proposed the adoption of a communistic society, to be commenced by the communal farming of the common and waste lands of England. In every case, these manifestations of radicalism met with state oppression and social stigmatism. As movements essentially embracing segments of England's discontented proletariat, they failed to provide the desired relief for the betterment of man's estate or the fulfilment of basic psycho-religious needs.

The fulfilment of those needs came for many in the lower classes through the spiritualistically-oriented teaching of the sectaries. In the age of revolution they represented the fag end of the religious revolution launched by Luther over a century earlier. Unsatisfied with the rigidity and ritual of a state church —be it Anglican or Presbyterian—they sought religious satisfaction in independent congregations of saints. There, enthusiasm replaced formality, and the Spirit, so they believed, was free to work as it wished. There too was the breeding ground for much of the rampant anti-professionalism which continued unabated throughout the 1650's. Ordained ministers, lawyers, university professors, and even medical practitioners were subjected to withering criticism by the sectaries. It was in those congregations of saints that the movement for the supremacy of the lay mind gained impetus.[1] Barred by society from high political, economic, intellectual, and social attainment, tinkers and farmers, mechanics and day labourers could find in the sectarian churches a distinct spiritual superiority. That superiority, based on the free working of the Spirit in whom it will, psychologically compensated for all the more materialistic frustrations of life. It was more than a panacea which religion provided for them; it was a firm conviction of spiritual supremacy and sainthood in the present.

The historian is provided with a wealth of sectarian literature. That literature recorded for posterity the essence of the sectarian message which so appealed to many of those Englishmen who suffered most in the century of revolution. From those writings can be constructed the basic concepts which many of the generally inarticulate classes of England embraced to satisfy their psychological and religious needs. Many of these concepts were shared with the Puritans, whose preaching found wide acceptance among members of the middle class and gentry. Yet other concepts marked the sectaries as men who carried the religious revolution one step beyond Puritanism in their quest to discover inner satisfaction and—unconsciously—to compensate for the frustrations born out of class distinctions. The theological message they proclaimed is well represented in the prolific writings of the preacher and tinker, John Bunyan.

The Life of John Bunyan

BUNYAN'S life[2] spanned that tumultuous period of English history extending from the Petition of Right of 1628 to the Glorious Revolution of 1688. His parents, Thomas and Margaret Bunyan, were relatively poor residents of Elstow, Bedfordshire, where Bunyan was baptised on 30 November 1628. Bunyan himself, in his spiritual autobiography *Grace Abounding to the Chief of Sinners* (1666), gave virtually the only reliable information known about his scanty education. There he observed that he had been taught "both to Read and Write; the which I also attained, according to the rate of other poor mens children . . .", though he never advanced "to Aristotle or Plato".[3] After the completion of his education he became an apprentice to his father and learned the trade of a brazier.

In his youth Bunyan underwent an astonishing variety of religious experiences, the key element in which was the traumatic perception of a God who "did scare and affright me with fearful dreams, and did terrifie me with dreadful visions." Still, the hand of God was occasionally felt in mercy as well as in awesome judgement. His psychological state was further disrupted in 1644, the year of Marston Moor, when his mother and sister died.

Within a month of his sister's death, he was rudely shocked by his father's remarriage—an act which must have seemed to violate the canons of decency and abiding love. In less than a year, probably during the autumn or winter of 1644, he joined the Parliamentary army. By the following June the battle of Naseby had decided the fate of the Royalist cause, but Bunyan himself had been exposed to a new world as a sixteen-year-old soldier. "It must have had an overwhelming effect on a youthful imagination to turn from the traditional, unintellectual Protestantism of Elstow to the fiery opinions of the preaching captains of Cromwell's Ironsides." From those captains as well as from the troopers themselves Bunyan must have become acquainted with "the prime notion of the enthusiastic sectaries . . . that the effort to religious truth meant an obstinate search, often from sect to sect, relying on free grace internally revealed, and condemning all forms of organisation as 'legal and dark'. . . ."[4]

Whatever impact his experience with sectarian notions in the army had upon Bunyan is not immediately discernible. By the summer of 1647 he had been discharged from the army. Several years later he married the daughter of a devout Protestant. From his father-in-law Bunyan received two books which, he wrote, "beget within me some desires to Religion. . . ."[5] The two books, the Calvinist and pietistic ideas of which are reflected in his own writings, were Arthur Dent's *The Plaine Mans Path-Way to Heauen* (1601) and Lewis Bayly's *The Practise of Pietie* (1613).

During the first four years or so of his married life Bunyan underwent a psychologically-trying period of despair which found him trudging through the Slough of Despond, "that despairing sense of sin through which he more than most men had to make his way to the better life." For a time he was devoutly religious, but then the simple act of playing the game of "cat" on Sunday afternoons brought on a period of intense anguish. Like any conscientious Puritan or sectary, he was grieved that he had violated the Sabbath, but unlike most other men a simple sin triggered another traumatic experience. Despairing of his sin he decided to sin all the more, and "the marvellous force which in after years displayed itself in vividness

of spiritual vision and burning power of expression ran riot in
weird blasphemies which made even blasphemers tremble". A
turning point of a sort came when the rebuke of "a very loose
and ungodly Wretch" caused him to turn once again to a fervent
religious life. But still he missed the wicket gate which would
bring peace to his troubled mind.[6]

Bunyan and Bedford

AN important moment in Bunyan's life came when, "upon a
day, the good Providence of God did cast me to Bedford. . . ."
There he overheard a small group of Christian women sharing
their religious experiences together. The effect on the troubled
Bunyan was enlightening: "me thought they spake as if joy did
make them speak. . . ." Convinced anew of his evil nature, he
sought again for deliverance from his doubts and fearful apprehensions. In his quest he came into contact with the tenets of the
Ranters, a fringe group indicative of the extremes to which
religious radicalism went in the mid-seventeenth century. The
Ranters were an Antinomian sect which stressed total reliance
on the inner revelatory workings of the Spirit to the exclusion of
the authority of Scripture and ministry. Bunyan did not find the
answers he sought in these beliefs. Comfort and temptation now
began to follow one another with distressing frequency, and life
for the troubled tinker became a dizzy see-sawing between hope
and despair. His disquieted psychological state was further per-
turbed by a dream in which he perceived that the narrow entrance
to the church precluded any sin. A "sound sense of Death, and of
the Day of Judgement" continually filled his mind as a result of
this dream.[7]

By now events in revolutionary England had moved swiftly,
bringing an abrupt end to the monarchy and the House of Lords.
Of these events Bunyan pays no heed in his autobiography. To
him all that was momentous and significant was happening within
his disturbed mind. The Commonwealth was two or three years

old when he first began to attend the services of the Separatist church at Bedford. That church had been founded as recently as 1650, and had called as its first pastor John Gifford. Bunyan later wrote that Gifford's preaching "was much for my stability".[8]

It was in these tumultuous years for Bunyan that he also became acquainted with the writing of Luther, which cast an indelible imprint upon his concept of Christianity. What he read was Luther's commentary on Paul's epistle to the Galatians. Like Luther, Bunyan's quest for religious peace was a momentous psychological experience, though the identity crisis suggested to be the root of Luther's experience is to be replaced by a distinctly psychopathic temperament in Bunyan's case. Bunyan was "beset by doubts, fears, and insistent ideas, and a victim of verbal automatisms, both motor and sensory." What is certain is that Bunyan recognised an immediate spiritual kinship with the German reformer. "When I had but a little way perused [the commentary]," he wrote, "I found my condition, in his experience, so largely and profoundly handled, as if his Book had been written out of my heart. . . ." That which he found particularly revealing was Luther's treatment of the temptations which afflict man, "namely, Blasphemy, Desparation, and the like; shewing that the Law of Moses, as well as the Devil, Death and Hell, hath a very great hand therein. . . ." Luther's impact was so great on Bunyan that the latter recommended Luther's commentary as "most fit for a wounded Conscience".[9]

The inner storm was nearly abated. The end of the ordeal brought for Bunyan, as it had for Luther, a serene calm. To Bunyan came an assuring sense of "those heights and depths in grace, and love, and mercy," and the life-long conviction that "great sins do draw out great grace; and where guilt is most terrible and fierce, there the mercy of God in Christ . . . appears most high and mighty. . . ." So real to him was this forgiving grace that the mystically transcendental nearly obliterated the mundane: "I had two or three times, at or about my deliverance from this temptation such strange apprehensions of the Grace of God, that I could hardly bear up under it, it was so out of measure amazing, when I thought it could reach me, that I do think, if that sense of it had abode long upon me, it would have made me uncapable for business."[10]

Bunyan became a member of Gifford's church in 1653. That same year Gifford was presented to the living of the parish church of St. John's at Bedford, hence Bunyan's first years of church life were spent as a member of the broadly-inclusive Cromwellian state church. Gifford was held in high esteem by Bunyan, a fact which is reflected in the role assigned by Bunyan to Evangelist in *The Pilgrim's Progress*. Gifford died two years later, in 1655, and was replaced as rector by John Burton. Shortly thereafter the congregation invited Bunyan to preach, and doing so he found that his oratorical abilities provoked a favourable response from his audience. Burton's frequent periods of illness resulted in further opportunities for Bunyan to explore his facility to preach. When further testimonies of edification ensued from his listeners, Bunyan was "more particularly called forth, and appointed to a more ordinary and publick preaching [of] the Word. . . ." In the typical empirical tradition of the sectaries, the essence of his message was grounded in his personal experience: "I preached what I felt, what I smartingly did feel. . . ." It was that authoritative voice of experience which lent the kind of credence to his message which appealed to the unsophisticated but fervent seeker for religious certainty.[11]

Bunyan in Conflict

PUBLIC preaching soon gave rise to public debates, especially by means of the printed word, with the Quakers. Their thorough-going reliance on the Inner Light was no more acceptable to Bunyan than were the tenets of the Ranters, essentially because the more literal-minded Bunyan insisted on the objective character of revelation. As part of his early debates with the Quakers, a creation of the Civil War era, Bunyan published his first book—a polemic against Quaker teaching entitled *Some Gospel-Truths Opened according to the Scriptures*. The theme of the work was the advocacy of the historicity of the life and death of Jesus against what Bunyan felt was the extreme spiritualising of this historicity by the Quakers. The latter's defence was undertaken by the young Quaker polemicist Edward Burrough (1634–1662), in *The True Faith of the Gospel of Peace Contended for, in the Spirit of Meekness* (1656). The two men exchanged views again in two tracts published the following year. Bunyan's first non-controversial work, *A Few Sighs from Hell, or, the Groans of a Damned Soul*, appeared in 1658, the year of Cromwell's death. A year later he published his first book of major importance, a theological tract which none of his later writings in a similar vein surpassed. The book was entitled *The Doctrine of the Law and Grace Unfolded*.

Bunyan's lack of formal education as preparation for the ministry bothered him not at all, for he thoroughly embraced the general sectarian regard for the sufficiency of spiritual enlightenment for the ministry. Others, including the Puritans, were of a different mind. On Christmas day, 1659, Bunyan preached in the pulpit of the leading sectary William Dell (d. 1669), rector of Yelden, Bedfordshire, and Master of Caius College, Cambridge. That sermon provoked an attack on Bunyan's right to preach by Thomas Smith, the Professor of Arabic and University Librarian at Cambridge. Smith warned that Englishmen must not "think a Tinker more infall[i]ble then the pure Spouse of Christ. . . ."[12] On this occasion Bunyan's right to preach was defended by a fellow sectary, the Baptist Henry Denne (d. 1660?).

Throughout his life Bunyan gloried in the opposition to his work and thought. From the very beginning his critics enabled him to play the coveted role of a martyr, which only added to his authority and effectiveness with his audiences. To the initial published criticism of his thought by Edward Burrough he confidently replied: "The Truth is of that nature, that the more it is opposed, the more glory it appears in; and the more the adversary objects against it, the more it will clear it self. . . ." Supremely confident—as all sectaries were—that he possessed the truth, Bunyan prepared the way for Christian to set out on his pilgrimage by admonishing the readers of the allegory to

> . . . let Truth be free
> To make her Salleys upon Thee, and Me,
> Which way it pleases God.

Such a Miltonesque passage evokes the image of a man whose basic convictions were strong enough to encounter successfully the most troublesome adversary.[13]

Bunyan had barely established himself as a lay preacher when his wife died in 1658. Although he remarried the following year, there was to be little time to enjoy the amenities of domestic life. The accession of Charles II to the throne in 1660 brought an end to the limited toleration of the Cromwellian era. The liberty for tender consciences promised in the Declaration of Breda never effectively materialised, as Bunyan quickly realised. In November, 1660, he was arrested for preaching in the hamlet of Lower Samsell, Bedfordshire. Prosecuted under an Elizabethan act against Nonconformity (35 Eliz. c. i), he was imprisoned in the county jail at Bedford for a period of three months, though this was eventually extended to a total of six years. During his confinement he supported himself and his family by making "long Tagg'd Laces," though he also found time to act as a religious counsellor to those permitted to visit him. On occasion throughout his imprisonment he was allowed to leave the jail for brief periods of time. Much of the time in prison was spent writing, at least nine books being written during these six years. Among them was his spiritual autobiography, *Grace Abounding*.[14]

A brief respite from imprisonment came in 1666, but before the year was ended Bunyan had been put back into prison for another six years. During this period he attempted a refutation of Edward Fowler's *The Design of Christianity* (1671). Fowler (1632–1714), the future Bishop of Gloucester, was currently vicar of Northill, Bedfordshire, and was taken to task by Bunyan in the latter's *A Defence of the Doctrine of Justification, by Faith in Jesus Christ* (1672). A more extensive controversy was carried on between Bunyan and various sectaries of Baptist persuasion. This debate was triggered by the publication of his *Confession of My Faith, and a Reason of My Practice* (1672), which advocated the principle of open membership and communion. Before the controversy ended in 1674 Bunyan had written two additional defences of his position, and had been taken to task by Baptists Thomas Paul (*fl.* 1673), John Denne (d. 1676?), William Kiffin (1616–1701), and Henry Danvers (d. 1687).

In 1672 Bunyan was finally released from prison, and in the same year he was chosen pastor of the Bedford Separatist church. The church minutes for 21 January, 1672 report:

> At a full assembly of the Church at Bedford the 21th of the 10th month. After much seeking God by prayer, and sober conference formerly had, the Congregation did at this meeting with joynt consent (signifyed by solemne lifting up of their hands) call forth and appoint our bro: John Bunyan to the pastorall office, or elder-ship; And he accepting thereof gave up himself to serve Christ, and his church in that charge; and received of the elders the right hand of fellowship.

In May of the same year Bunyan took advantage of the opportunity presented by Charles II's politically expedient Declaration of Indulgence to have himself licensed as a teacher of a Congregational church. Such a licence has been cited as proof that Bunyan adhered to the Congregational tradition. Yet in a work published posthumously he referred to the Anabaptists and remarked that "I go under that name my self". It is, in fact, pointless to attempt to identify him as either a thorough-going Baptist or a staunch Congregationalist in the light of his liberal views on the subject of baptism and church membership. When his Baptist critics pressed him to declare to which group he actually belonged, Bunyan replied: "Since you would know by what Name I would be distinguished from others; I tell you, I would be, and hope I am, a Christian. . . ."[15]

From the end of his imprisonment in 1672 until his death on 31 August, 1688, Bunyan spent his time preaching and writing, though he was also imprisoned for a short time in the Bedford city jail in 1675–76. It was in this period that his greatest literary works were published, including *The Pilgrim's Progress* (1678 and 1684), *The Life and Death of Mr. Badman* (1680), and *The Holy War* (1682). Throughout these years his preaching centred on the theme of the abundance of divine grace for sinners, and in one of his last works he informed his readers that he had found "good success in Preaching upon this Subject. . . ."[16] It was a very accurate self-appraisal of his work.

Sectary and Calvinist

BUNYAN'S place in the English Protestant movement can be distinguished in two different but complementary ways. He was, first of all, a sectary and not a Puritan. Traditionally Puritans had preferred the possibility of reforming the existing state church rather than separating from it, as did the sectaries. After the Restoration in 1660, however, Puritans such as Richard Baxter were forced by the dictates of their consciences to follow the Separatist path of nonconformity rather than remain a part of the neo-Stuart church. Bunyan, as will be shown, was distinctly a Separatist in his ecclesiological thought, and manifested no desire to remain within the Anglican Church to work for its "purification".

Theological views in some cases distinguished Puritans from sectaries. The Puritans were adherents of the Calvinist tradition, though occasionally defectors to Arminianism have been included within their ranks.[17] Theologically the sectaries were not of one mind, but variously embraced Antinomianism, mysticism, and some Arminianism as well as Calvinism. Bunyan himself, although not without certain Antinomian tendencies, customarily agreed with the Calvinists on the issues most basic to their theological system.

A major point of distinction between Puritans and sectaries concerned their epistemological views. The Puritans differed from the sectaries by retaining rationalism as a significant element in their religious epistemology. That rationalism was, however, subordinated to faith and empiricism, though Puritans were generally agreed that Spirit and reason were to be juxtaposed. The sectaries, on the other hand, could be distinguished from the Puritans by their religious anti-rationalism and anti-intellectualism. Bunyan himself made no attempt to apologise for his lack of formal education; instead, he specifically gloried in his relative ignorance because he believed it permitted the Spirit to work unhindered. There was definitely a certain sense of appeal to the uneducated when "a dull sounding Rams-horn," as he once described himself, boasted that "for my part, I am not ashamed to Confess, that I neither know the Mode nor Figure of a Sylogism, nor scarce which is Major or Minor." He specifically explained that the revelatory work of the Spirit through Scripture was sufficient for all religious knowledge, and coupled this with a warning against dependence on the much adored idol of university education. Even if he had such learning, he contended that he would refuse to use it "for fear lest that Grace, and those Gifts that the Lord hath given me, should be attributed to their Wits, rather then the Light of the Word and Spirit of God. . . ." Such a conception was quite foreign to the respect which Puritans had for the role of education in obtaining religious knowledge. As Baxter enunciated the Puritan position, "Education is God's ordinary way for the Conveyance of his Grace, and ought no more to be set in opposition to the Spirit, than the preaching of the Word. . . ."[18]

Bunyan's place in the English Protestant movement can also be distinguished on a more strictly theological basis. At the centre of the theological stream in mid-seventeenth century England were two groups of Calvinists, the first of which may be termed strict Calvinists, and the second, moderate Calvinists. It was the first group which more than any other most faithfully embodied the tenets of Calvin, even while making those tenets rigid canons of orthodoxy defined by the fine points of a new scholasticism. The moderate Calvinists adhered more closely to the Zwingli-Tyndale tradition, which had been a part of English theological thought since the Reformation.[19] Moving beyond this bipartite centre towards the ends of the continuum there were on the one hand the Antinomians, who blended with orthodox Calvinism certain of the more extreme elements in Luther's thought and various unorthodox conclusions derived in whole or in part from orthodox Calvinist premises. At the other end of the continuum were the Arminians, whose reaction to orthodox Calvinism was more pronounced than that of the moderate Calvinists. Bunyan himself, as this study will demonstrate, adhered essentially to those positions advocated by the strict Calvinists, though on occasion he demonstrated certain Antinomian leanings. Unlike most English writers of the seventeenth century, however, he was definitely indebted to the writings of Martin Luther for various emphases in his thought. Such emphases tended to give his own thought something of a hybrid character, combining Lutheran and Calvinist concepts with certain ideas drawn from Antinomianism and the Separatist tradition. In one way at least, this hybrid character of Bunyan's thought was significant: the emphases drawn from Luther gave his writing and preaching a more personal appeal than would have been the case had he relied solely on the more logic-bound orthodox Calvinism.

NOTES

[Place of Publication is London unless otherwise noted. Bunyan's works are designated by Roman numerals only; for their meaning see the Bibliography.]

1. Among those studies especially useful for describing these trends are James Fulton Maclear, "The Making of the Lay Tradition," *The Journal of Religion*, XXXIII (April, 1953), 113–136; Maclear, "Popular Anticlericalism in the Puritan Revolution," *Journal of the History of Ideas*, XVII (October, 1956), 443–470; Leo F. Solt, "Anti-Intellectualism in the Puritan Revolution, *Church History*, XXIV (December, 1956), 306–316; Richard Schlatter, "The Higher Learning in Puritan England," *Historical Magazine of the Protestant Episcopal Church*, XXIII (June, 1954), 167–187.
2. The best biographies are those of John Brown, *John Bunyan* (1628–1688): *His Life, Times, and Work* (Tercentenary ed., rev.

by F. M. Harrison, 1928); Roger Sharrock, *John Bunyan* (1954); Henri Talon, *John Bunyan: The Man and His Works*, trans. Barbara Wall (1951); and O. E. Winslow, *John Bunyan* (New York, 1961). Also useful is W. Y. Tindall, *John Bunyan: Mechanick Preacher* (New York, 1934).

3. XVI, sect. 3; XII, fol. B1.

4. XVI, sect. 5; Sharrock, "Personal Vision & Puritan Tradition in Bunyan," *The Hibbert Journal*, LVI (October, 1957), 53–54; Sharrock, Introduction to *Grace Abounding* (Oxford, 1962 ed.), p. xv.

5. XVI, sect. 12.

6. Brown, *John Bunyan*, pp. 55, 57; XVI, sect. 22.

7. XVI, sects. 28, 29; XVII, sect. 70.

8. XVI, sect. 96. For a history of this church see *The Church Book of Bunyan Meeting, 1650–1821*, ed. G. B. Harrison (1928); and H. G. Tibbutt, *Bunyan Meeting, Bedford, 1650–1950* (Bedford, n.d.).

9. Erik H. Erikson, *Young Man Luther: A Study in Psychoanalysis and History* (New York, 1958); William James, *The Varieties of Religious Experience* (1929), p. 157; XVII, sects. 130–31.

10. XVI, sect. 206; XVII, sect. 253.

11. XVI, sects. 221, 229.

12. *The Quaker Disarm'd* (1659), fol. D1.

13. XL, p. 23; XXVIII, fol. A6.

14. For a complete listing of Bunyan's works see F. M. Harrison, *A Bibliography of the Works of John Bunyan* (Oxford, 1932).

15. *Church Book*, pp. 50–51; *Original Records of Early Nonconformity under Persecution and Indulgence*, ed. G. L. Turner (1911), II, 855; XIX, p. 15; LIX, Vol. II, 103.

16. XV, fol. A3 *verso*.

17. See, e.g., Geoffrey F. Nuttall, *The Holy Spirit in Puritan Faith and Experience* (Oxford, 1946).

18. XXV, p. 251; IV, p. 8; XX, fols. A2 *verso*, A6–A6 *verso*; Baxter, *Reliquiae Baxterianae*, ed. M. Sylvester (1696), Bk. I, pt. 1, sect. 6 (p. 7).

19. See Richard L. Greaves, "The Origins and Early Development of English Covenant Thought," *The Historian*, XXXI (November 1968), 21—35.

1 The Pilgrim's God

GOD, AS HE WAS REVEALED to Bunyan through the work of the Spirit, was a complex being whose sovereign majesty could be manifested as wrath or as grace, as justice or as mercy. What particularly concerned Bunyan, as well as all other Christian pilgrims, was the nature of their relationship to this awesome, nearly foreboding being. Before the character of this relationship could be properly understood, the serious pilgrim regarded it as essential to grasp something of the nature of God. Then, having become aware of the rudiments of that nature, he could understand something of the way in which divine love and mercy were extended to him through the life and death of Jesus. For it was that work of grace which was, for the pilgrim, the basis of his relationship with God. The nature of God and the atonement were therefore essential to a correct understanding of the pilgrim's salvation and life in this world.

The Divine as Wrath and Grace

WHEN the good Prince Emanuel had thus beleaguered Mansoul: In the first place he hangs out the White Flag, which he caused to be set up among the Golden slings that were planted upon Mount Gracious. And this he did for two reasons: 1. To give notice to Mansoul that he could and would yet be gracious if they turned to him. 2. And that he might leave them the more without excuse, should he destroy them, they continuing in their rebellion . . .[1]

Then he commanded, and they set the Red Flag, upon that Mount called Mount Justice. 'Twas the Red Flag of Captain Judgment, whose Scutcheon was the Burning Fiery Furnace.[1]

The polarity implied by Bunyan in his allegorical usage of Mount Gracious and Mount Justice was derived from his personal religious experience as described on page after page of *Grace Abounding to the Chief of Sinners*. At the same time this polarity was also distinctly reminiscent of Luther's diametrically opposed concepts of divine anger and grace as he depicted them throughout his commentary on Galatians. What Bunyan learned from this commentary and from his religious experience he combined with prolix biblical exegesis to develop his concept of the nature of God.

Bunyan at least theoretically resolved the apparent irreconcilability of such attributes as justice and mercy, holiness and love. In terms of theological rationale—if not always of experience—these attributes were said to be 'without Division; one Glorious and eternal Being'. This he made explicit:

No man must conceive of God, as if he consisted of these Attributes, as our Body doth of its Members, one standing here, another there, for the compleating personal Subsistence: For though by the Word we may distinguish, yet may we not divide them, or presume to appoint them their places in the Godhead: Wisdom is in his Justice, Holiness is in his Power, Justice is in his Mercy, Holiness is in his Love, Power is in his Goodness.

The various divine attributes thus permeated one another in actuality, though in appearance they appeared to be distinct and even essentially contradictory. One of Bunyan's spiritual progenitors, Lewis Bayly, had posed virtually the same argument when he had written that 'the Essentiall Attributes of God differ not Essentially, nor really one from another . . . but onely in our reason and vnderstanding . . . '.[2]

Generally speaking, Bunyan's concept of God was that which had been taught in the Christian church for centuries. The differences which had developed were mostly differences of emphasis rather than differences of substance. This was particularly true within the Protestant tradition. Those notably influenced by Luther tended to discuss the nature of God primarily in terms of the wrath-grace dichotomy, whereas the impact of Calvin tended to produce more of a concern with the divine will and omnipotence. Most writers in the Puritan tradition were imbued with Calvinist influence in their doctrine of God, but men such as Bunyan and, to a certain extent, Thomas Goodwin, were influenced by Luther's more personal and dichotomous God. The key to Bunyan's acceptance of Luther's concept of God[3] rather than the more prevalent Calvinist concept was the similarity of Bunyan's and Luther's religious experiences. For Bunyan as for Luther, religion always remained intensely experiential and barely intellectual. Calvinism, on the other hand, although not without its experiential element, more readily lent itself to an intellectual interpretation. Certainly an intensely religious personality such as Bunyan's could more easily identify itself with Luther's struggle with a God of wrath and grace than it could with the Calvinist God of predestination.

In his commentary on Galatians Luther had cautioned his readers that "true Christian divinity . . . commandeth us not to search out the nature of God . . .," explicitly warning them that there was "nothing more dangerous then to wander with curious speculations in heaven, & there to search out God in his incomprehensible power, wisdome and Majesty. . . ."[4] This admonition was generally heeded by Bunyan, who observed of such attributes as holiness, justice, and mercy, that God was "inconceivably perfect and infinite, not to be comprehended by things in Earth, or things in Heaven. . . ."[5] Consequently at no point in his writings did Bunyan make a systematic, concerted attempt to discuss the divine nature. In this respect he was a typical sectary. Yet even the sectaries had their ideas about God's nature, even if those ideas were never systematically developed as various of the Puritans developed them.

For Bunyan the divine nature was holiness, and that holiness was believed to pervade all the attributes of God. Such holiness, being absolute purity, was in large measure responsible for generating in man a fear of God. Bunyan himself reflected the same fear as that experienced by Luther when he experientially observed that "the Name of God is dreadful to us, specially when he is discovered to us by those names that declare his Justice, Holiness, Power, and Glory. . . ." Never was any man more gripped by this fear than when he became aware of his own evil and impure nature. The resulting dread which a man of the seventeenth century might experience was the direct result of his belief in the eschatological implications of divine holiness for the unrepentant sinner:

> . . . God as he is Love,
> So he is Justice, therefore cannot move,
> Or in the least be brought to favour those,
> His Holiness and Justice doth oppose.

Seriously to consider the holiness of God in these terms could thus strike terror into the mind of a receptive individual. It was an unnerving experience for such a person to be confronted with the awful warning that divine holiness would "not give way for such unclean wretches to abide in his sight. . . ."[6]

Justice, too, was, for Bunyan, the very essence of God. He would not have agreed with Thomas Goodwin that this justice was less natural to God than his mercy.[7] Rather he persistently maintained that God was justice as well as mercy, which meant that salvation for a pilgrim had to be "by Law as well as Grace. That is, in a way of Justice as well as . . . Mercy".[8] Bunyan's interest in divine justice was in terms of its relationship to man as a sinner; his interest thus reflected the preoccupation which Luther had manifested with soteriology. Bunyan was not concerned about the controversy between fellow Calvinists and Arminians over the relation of the divine will to justice.[9] Instead, he considered his belief that justice demanded the punishment of sin and the rendering by the sinner (or a suitable substitute) of due satisfaction for it. "Justice calls for satisfaction . . .," he wrote, in order that there be, as Baxter explained it, no "diminution of his Honour or Justice. . . ." Personalising the ordinarily abstract concept of justice, Bunyan cautioned his readers that "justice once offended, knoweth not how to shew any pitty [*sic*] or compassion to the offender . . .," and will cause him to suffer eternally "unless infinite satisfaction be given to it. . . ."[10]

The dreadfulness of this justice was particularly manifest—as it was with holiness—when it had an eschatological reference. Although Bunyan preferred to speak of the glorification of justice in relation to salvation rather than eternal punishment, he nevertheless made the ensign of Captain Execution, whose escutcheon was a fruitless tree with an axe at its root, Mr. Justice, thus implying the relation of justice to future judgment. He could not stress enough "with what delight he [i.e., God] will burn sinners in the flames of Hell, for the easing of his mind, and the satisfaction of his Justice". Bunyan did not write this with a vindictive spirit; it came as an honest warning from one who deeply believed that "Justice has measures and rules to go by; unto which measures and rules, if thou com'st not up, Justice can do thee no good". Grace notwithstanding, "Justice must be distributed with equity". These were chilling words, designed to strike fear into the minds of listeners or readers, prompting them to strive towards a better life.[11]

Bunyan defined the wrath of God as the execution of divine justice.[12] Wrath was likened to consuming fire and spoken of as vengeance. Bunyan made no attempt to distinguish between chastising anger and avenging wrath, as did various other writers.[13] He was concerned only with warning his fellow man that divine wrath abode on the unrepentant sinner because of his sinful nature; hence man as well as sin was the object of that terrible wrath. The ultimate choice offered by God to man was solely between wrath and grace; precisely because of this alternative wrath too achieved its basic importance in Bunyan's thought when seen in relation to man's ultimate destiny.

Since the God of grace was also the God of wrath, Bunyan's God could say to those who remained unrepentant:

My dreadful Wrath shall follow you apace;
Into Eternal Fire now do you fall.

Upon such unrepentant sinners "the wrath of God shall smoke to their eternal ruine". It was the fear of such wrath which drove both Luther and Bunyan to seek forgiveness of sins by the grace of God. Yet even after Bunyan experienced this forgiveness, the awfulness of such wrath remained impressed indelibly on his mind. The haunting question persisted: "If the very looks of God be so terrible, what will his blows be? . . ."[14] It is not difficult to understand how an intense awareness of this judgement-minded, fiery God of wrath and justice could give rise to psychological aberrations in a sensitive mind. Yet the Puritans and sectaries customarily balanced this picture by holding forth hope of divine love, mercy, and grace.

God's love was experientially sensed and described just as his wrath and justice had been. Thomas Goodwin, for example, asserted that the difference between divine and human love was "found more by tasting, and by feeling of it, than it is by setting of it forth; as it is in Wines. . . ."[15] In the same vein Bunyan wrote that the love of God was "better felt and enjoyed, then talked of". Later in his ministry, however, he felt it necessary to caution his readers against an excessive reliance on feeling. His principle was that "love ought to be considered with reference to the subject [i.e., God] as well as to the object of it". Such a statement reflected the delicate balance which he attempted to maintain between a theology too closely bound by the coldness of objective reasoning on the one hand, and by unbridled emotional enthusiasm on the other.[16]

For Bunyan love was the very nature and essence of God. Love was so essential to the divine being that there was a tendency in Bunyan's thought to resolve all the divine attributes into love: "God is love; might some say, and Justice too: but his Justice is turned with Wisdom, Power, Holiness and Truth, to love, yea, to love those that he found in his Son. . . ." Thomas Goodwin, too, affirmed that "all the Attributes in God, they are subjected to his Love. . . ." For Bunyan, as for other writers, this love, along with mercy and grace, was an expression of God's essential goodness. Bunyan would have readily concurred with Thomas Goodwin's reference to such goodness as "the Fountain of Love in God".[17]

Bunyan did not speak of love in terms of the divine will as did
Calvinists such as Bayly, John Owen, and James Ussher.[18] This
did not, however, mean that for Bunyan love lacked requisite
power, for it was depicted as acting "of and from it self, without
. . . dependencies". In other words, the rather impersonal will of
God which dominated traditional Calvinist thought was replaced
in importance in Bunyan's thought by the more personal love of
God. Here he was closer to the Wittenberg reformer than to the
Genevan scholar. The real importance of divine love for Bunyan
was its relation to soteriology—to the ultimate salvation of the
pilgrim. He continually emphasised that it was this love which
was the foundation of salvation, or as fellow sectary John Saltmarsh phrased it, that which "began all the work of salvation in
God. . . ." Its greatness, as Christian pilgrims had always testified,
was profoundly expressed in the bestowal of the divine Son as a
redeemer.[19]

Mercy was not described by Bunyan as being either the divine
nature itself or an essential property in God. Such descriptions
were, however, made by contemporary Calvinists.[20] Bunyan
depicted God's mercy primarily in terms of compassion, pity,
"tender-heartednesse", "a feeling of the Condition of those in
misery", and "a running over of infinite Bowels to objects in a
miserable and helpless condition". It had a special reference to the
miserable state in which fallen man existed—a state which evoked
compassionate pity from man's maker. Very similar was Thomas
Goodwin's conception of divine mercy as "a Disposition to shew
Pity, and to relieve one in Misery. . . ." Owen broadened this
commonly-accepted concept of mercy by defining it as the
"Goodness, Kindness, and Benignity of God in Christ".[21]

Bunyan did not follow the Calvinist tendency to associate
closely mercy and the divine will, nor was he willing to accept
the Calvinist idea (as expressed here by Arthur Dent) that mercy
was "restrained onely to the elect. . . ."[22] Instead Bunyan asserted
that all men were to some extent recipients of the mercy of God.
At the same time, however, such mercy was most fully manifest
in God's bestowal of his Son as a redeemer. It was precisely this
relation of mercy to salvation which made it so significant:

"Mercy is the original, the cause, and the manager of our redemption. Redemption is the manifestation, and the compleating of that Mercy. If there had been no Mercy, there had been no redemption. . . ."[23] It was thus not with mercy as it was an attribute or property of God that Bunyan was concerned, but with mercy as it was a basis of soteriology.

The concept of the grace of God expressed in Bunyan's writings consistently mirrored his own experience of conversion and the Christian life. "There is nothing in Heaven or Earth," he wrote shortly before his death, "that can so Awe the heart, as the Grace of God. 'Tis that which makes a Man fear, 'tis that which makes a Man tremble, 'tis that which makes a Man bow and bend, and break to pieces".[24] When he spoke of grace, it was almost always in terms of its relation between God and man rather than as a divine attribute or the nature of God.

Grace itself was described in a variety of ways by Bunyan, and these descriptions were paralleled in the writings of his contemporaries: good will, the good pleasure of God's will, or a free act of his will; free love; loving-kindness; goodness; and free mercy.[25] Bunyan's basic understanding of grace was as God's good will (or the good pleasure of his will), and free love. This grace was both free and sovereign: "Grace, shews that God by all that he doth towards us in saving and forgiving, acts freely as the highest Lord and of his own good will and pleasure. . . ." Such freeness and sovereignty provide the key to the difference between mercy and grace, for whereas mercy implied pity to one in a state of misery, grace signified that "God still acts in this as a free agent, not being wrought upon by the misery of the creature, as a procuring cause; but of his own princely mind". In spite of its freeness, however, grace could not, according to Bunyan, be extended to man in a way contrary to divine justice. Hence there was the necessity for a redeemer, and it was God's grace which "moved him to give Christ a Ransom for sinners. . . ."[26]

The pilgrim's God as depicted by Bunyan could be a very terrifying or a very comforting figure. Men were reminded that God was justice as well as love, and therefore that there could be no favouring of those whom his holiness and justice opposed.

Grace and mercy could not operate in contradiction to holiness and justice. The latter demanded the execution of wrath upon those who had transgressed, and that included all men. Hence a way had to be found for a loving God to treat repentant man mercifully and graciously without doing violence to divine holiness and justice. The solution, as Bunyan and his contemporaries described it, was the atonement performed by Christ.

The Divine Extension of Grace

MANSOUL is mine by right of purchase. I have bought it (O Diabolus) I have bought it to my self. . . .

Nor did I do this to the halves, my Fathers Law and Justice that were both concerned in the threatning upon transgression, are both now satisfied, and very well content that Mansoul should be delivered.

That which prompted Emmanuel to purchase Mansoul, "the Argument that prevailed with Christ to do this great service for Man, [was] the Grace that was in his heart. . . ." If it was grace on the part of the Son that made the atonement possible, it was no less the grace of the Father which "moved him to give Christ a Ransom for sinners. . . ." Grace, then, was the foundation of the atonement. Yet without Christ, Bunyan contended, there would have been no bestowal of grace upon man at all.[27]

For Bunyan the importance of the role which Christ fulfilled in bringing the grace of God to the sinner could not be questioned. It was impossible, as Saltmarsh phrased it, "in a Scripture-way [to] consider any act of grace from God but in the Son. . . ." Consequently God had, to quote Bunyan again, "made way for his grace to come to us through the sides, and the heart Blood of his well beloved Son. . . ." Christ himself was thus the revelation of this divine grace, the one "from whom, by, or through whom the Grace of God doth come to us". Hence Bunyan described Christ as "the inlet to saving grace. . . ."[28]

The manifestation of grace in Christ was based on the idea that in the person of Christ God was in "union and communion" with man, so that Christ could be said to be "fellow [with God] in his mercy and grace. . . ." The condescending nature of this grace was especially revealed to man by the Son's leaving heaven for the humbleness of earth, and the giving of his life for sinners:

> What Grace was manifest in thy Condescention? Grace brought thee down from Heaven, Grace stript thee of thy Glory, Grace made thee Poor and Despicable, Grace made thee bear such burdens of Sin. . . . Grace was in all thy Tears, Grace came bubling out of thy side with thy Blood. . . .

Grace was also manifest by Christ when he commanded his disciples to offer salvation to the people of Jerusalem—"the biggest Sinners"—first. Christ, Bunyan wrote, had "all Grace perfect in him. . . ."[29]

The Necessity of Satisfaction

THE necessity of an atonement was based by Bunyan upon the assumption that grace could only be extended to the sinner in a way which was not contradictory to divine justice, hence the rhetorical question was asked: "If the Promise, and God's Grace without Christ's Blood would have saved us, wherefore then did Christ die?" For Bunyan there could be no thought of even the *theoretical* possibility that God could be gracious and merciful to sinners without an atonement for their sins. Thomas Goodwin, on the other hand, conjectured that God "might if he had pleased have ran a way and course of meer Mercy not temper'd with Justice at all, he might have pardoned without satisfaction. . . ." Goodwin could make such a statement on the basis of the importance which, as a Calvinist, he attached to the omnipotent divine will. But Bunyan, though a Calvinist himself, would not even admit the possibility of divine pardon without satisfaction.

When Edward Fowler made an opposite assertion, he was attacked by Bunyan in his *Defence of . . . Iustification, by Faith*. Since God was eternally just, Bunyan queried, "how can he Pardon without he be presented with that Satisfaction for Sin, that to all points of the highest perfection doth answer the Demands of this Infinite, and Eternal Justice?"[30]

The nature of an atonement which would reconcile grace and justice in the salvation of the sinner was one which of necessity provided full satisfaction for sin. Satisfaction was defined by Bunyan as doing "no more than compleatly to answer a legal Demand for harms and injuries done".[31] Bunyan insistently affirmed that a redeemer "must answer Divine Justice, or God must lye in saving them without inflicting the Punishment threatned;" or again, that "the justice of God is so pure, that if it be not compleatly satisfied in every particular, it giveth nothing but curses. . . ." The death of Christ thus had to appease the wrath of God.[32]

There were, however, those who dissented from the opinions of "the Satisfactionists, as the quaking Pen[n] is pleased to call them. . . ." William Penn (1644–1718) himself may be taken as an example of Quaker opposition to the doctrine of satisfaction as "inconsistent with the Dignity of God, and very repugnant to the Conditions, Nature, and Tendency of the second Covenant. . . ." Because God was gracious, merciful, and forgiving, Penn reasoned, it was consistent with his nature to remit man's sins "without any other consideration than his own Love; otherwise he could not justly come under the imputation of so many gracious Attributes, with whom it is impossible to pardon, and necessary to exact the payment of the utmost farthing".[33]

Such a position was wholly unacceptable to Bunyan, although he did little more to criticise such Quaker teaching, at least in print, than append to his *Defence of . . . Iustification, by Faith* a list of eight errors—three of which relate to satisfaction—in which he compared the teaching of Fowler with that of Penn. Penn had argued that the remission of sins was grounded on the sinner's repentance rather than a plenary satisfaction offered to God by Christ, and Fowler acknowledged that God could have pardoned sin on the basis of repentance alone, though he denied that God had done so. For Bunyan, both men were equally wrong. To assert the sufficiency of the sinner's repentance, he argued, was to say "that Man is, or may be in himself, just, that is, equal with God; or that the sin of Man was not a transgression of the Law that was given, and a procurer of the Punishment that is threat-[e]ned, by that Eternal God that gave it". Without the slightest intention to diminish grace, Bunyan insisted that "our Salvation is grounded on Justice, because merited by Blood".[34]

For other schools of thought which tended to reject his belief in the necessity of satisfaction, Bunyan likewise had little patience. He regarded damnation as the end of the Socinian who denied that Christ had rendered satisfaction to God. In his initial literary endeavours against the Quakers, Bunyan attacked their teaching that the church was redeemed from the curse of the law "by something that is done within them . . .," querying that if this was the case, why did Christ die? The misunderstanding involved in this controversy was apparent in the answer he received from Edward Burrough. The church, Burrough replied, was "redeemed by Christ Jesus which is revealed within all that believe. . . ." Burrough did not deny that salvation was completely accomplished by Christ. Where he decisively differed from Bunyan on the subject of the atonement was in his belief that Christ died—not to give satisfaction to God—but "because they wickedly judged him to be a blasphemer, and through their envy persecuted him to death, because he bore witnesse against them. . . ." Bunyan, on the other hand, was adamant throughout his writings that Christ died to give satisfaction to God for the sins of man against his law.[35]

According to Bunyan there was a definite relation between the atonement and divine law, for it was the law as well as justice which made satisfaction necessary. The satisfaction rendered to the law, Bunyan reasoned, could be "given to it, either by the mans own life, or by the blood of some other man. . . ." This was the position of the strict Calvinists, and was contrary to those who advocated that (in Baxter's words) "the satisfactoriness of Christ's sufferings . . . could not be the same which was due by the Law . . ."[36]

Now this division between strict Calvinists on the one hand and moderate Calvinists and Arminians on the other continued over the closely related question of whether or not Christ's sufferings were the literal penalty due to sinners. According to moderate Calvinists the punishment experienced by Christ was not the exact penalty owed to sinners; rather "the perfection of Christ's satisfaction . . . consisteth in its full sufficiency to those Ends for which it was designed . . .," namely the vindication of the law and lawgiver.[37] Strict Calvinists, on the other hand, contended that Christ suffered the identical penalty due to sinners. This Bunyan made explicit: "What ever the divine, infinite, and eternal justice of God did call for at the hands of man, . . . Jesus . . . did compleatly give a satisfaction to it. . . ."[38]

Sufficient satisfaction, according to Bunyan, demanded that Christ not only suffer the death due to sinners (his passive obedience), but also perfectly fulfil the law (his active obedience). It was both this active and passive obedience which was necessary to satisfy divine justice. "The obediential Righteousness of Jesus Christ," wrote Bunyan, was that "by which Gods Justice is satisfied. . . ." Elsewhere he explained that "this obediential Righteousness of Christ, consisteth of two parts: 1. In a doing of that which the Law commanded us to do. 2. In a paying that price for the transgression thereof, which Justice hath said shall be required at the hand of man; and that is the cursed death." It was essential that there be the "Perfection of Righteousness" in Christ's obedience to the law in order to render full satisfaction to the justice of God.[39] This again was the position of strict Calvinists, and was in sharp contrast to the Arminian assertion that Christ's passive obedience alone was sufficient to provide the necessary satisfaction to God.[40] The General Baptist John Denne, for example, in a critique of Bunyan's position, argued that "if Righteousness, Redemption, and Salvation had been performed by his personal acts [i.e., Christ's active obedience], there had then been no need of his Death and Passion. . . ."[41] The moderate Calvinists tried to find a *via media* between the strict Calvinist and Arminian positions by suggesting that it was the passive obedience of Christ which actually vindicated God's justice, but only as it was the fruit of his active obedience.[42]

Apart from those who denied the concept of satisfaction altogether, none would have quarrelled with Bunyan's statement that "infinite Justice cannot be satisfied with the recompence that Man can make. . . ." Hence the answer to the question, *Cur Deus homo?* Christ must first of all be man, since it was man that had offended God by sinning and was therefore necessitated by divine justice to make satisfaction. Yet Christ must also be God since "it was an infinite God that was transgressed against, and Justice required an infinite satisfaction, and therefore he must be infinite that must give this satisfaction, or else justice could not be satisfied. . . ." Because Christ was both God and man, he could therefore make the necessary satisfaction.[43]

The satisfaction which Christ made, Bunyan explained, was rendered by him not only as God and man, but also as a "Publick Person". As a public or common person Christ represented all "for whom he undertook thus to Live, and thus to die". Because Christ was such a public person, Bunyan concluded that he "stood before God in our Sins, and that God did not only suppose him so to stand, but set him in them, put them upon him, and count them as his own. . . ." This, said Bunyan, was an act of grace, and was "so true, that he cannot at present be a Christian that denies it". Nevertheless there were those—both moderate Calvinists and Arminians—who did deny it. Baxter, for example, was willing to acknowledge that Christ was man's "Publick Root", but he rejected the assertion that Christ undertook "what he did in our names, by representing our persons. . . ." Christ, Baxter argued, was made a sacrifice to atone for man's evil nature, but he never "was a Sinner indeed, or in Gods esteem. . . . Christ never undertook to be reputed of God one that was truly and formally wicked or a sinner. . . ."[44]

Bunyan did not believe the necessity of satisfaction in any way impinged upon the glory of divine grace, as did the Quakers and Socinians. Those who advocated some form of the satisfaction theory of the atonement would have concurred with Bunyan's declaration that Christ did not by becoming a means thorow death, of the conveyance of Grace to us, at all darken the nature or glory of Grace, but rather doth set it off the more. For wherein can Grace or Love more appear, than in his laying down his Life for us? I speak now of the Grace of the Son. And wherein could the nature and glory of grace of the Father more appear than in giving his Son to death for us, that grace might in a way of Justice as well as Mercy be bestowed upon the World?

Satisfaction and grace, as Thomas Goodwin summarised it, "may well stand together".[45]

The Extent of Grace

ONE of the most controversial theological questions of the seventeenth century related to the extent of the atonement, the crux of the issue being whether or not the grace of God was limited solely to the elect. Between those who firmly advocated that Christ died for all men, and those who were equally confident that he died for the elect alone, there were others who advocated various mediating theories. Among the principal debaters of this issue in Bunyan's lifetime were John Owen, who defended a limited atonement, John Goodwin, the most outstanding proponent of a general atonement, and Richard Baxter, who tried to reconcile the differences by asserting a mediatory position. Bunyan himself did not participate in the literary debate, hence in order to determine at what point he stood from what little he wrote on this issue, it is necessary to outline the principal positions.

The strict Calvinist position of a limited atonement was extensively developed in the writings of John Owen. "Christ did not dye," Owen wrote, "for any upon condition if they doe believe, but he died for all Gods elect, that they should believe, and believing have eternall life. . . ." One of the keys to his argument was the principle that "whatsoever Christ impetrated, merited, or obtained, by his death and passion, must be infallibly applied unto, and bestowed upon them, for whom he intended to obtaine it. . . ." Consequently he argued that if Christ died for all men, then all men must be saved. All men were not saved, however, *ergo* Christ did not die for all men, but for the elect alone. It was, however, said Owen, possible to say that Christ died for "all", but only in a very strict and limited sense: "first, in as much as the worth and value of his death, was very sufficient to have beene made a price for all their sinnes: secondly, in as much as this word All, is taken for some of all sorts, not for every one, of every sort. . . ."[46] For all practical purposes, however, the benefits of the atonement were strictly limited to the elect alone. No one else had even a remote possibility of sharing in those benefits. Those who adhered to such a position found it all the more impelling to find some psychological assurance that they were included among the elect.

In his attempt to mediate between the two extremes the moderate Calvinist Richard Baxter argued that Christ did indeed die for all men, though not for all equally, "or with the same intent, design or purpose. . . ."

> The conditional New Covenant, without any difference in the tenor of it, doth equally give Christ, Pardon and Life to all Mankind (antecedently to mens rejecting the offer) on condition of acceptance. And Christ equally satisfied Gods Justice for all the lapsed Race of Adam, so far as to procure them this Gift or Covenant, and the other foresaid common mercies: But not equally as to his Decree of the success: For there Election differenceth.

The problem of the extent of the atonement, therefore, was ostensibly resolved in terms of "Gods different Decrees about the effects of Redemption".[47] The net effect of such a position was to assert that Christ did die for all men, that the benefits of the atonement were generally available to all upon the same conditions of faith and repentance, but that only those actually predestined by God would fulfil the requisite conditions. In the end the results were the same; only the elect benefited from the atonement.

At the opposite extreme of Owen was his chief opponent in

the atonement debate, the Arminian John Goodwin. In his *magnum opus, Apolutrosis Apolutroseos or Redemption Redeemed,* Goodwin set forth an elaborate defence of "the Redemption of all Men by Christ, without exception. . . ." In saying this Goodwin was not asserting a doctrine of universalism, believing that all men would in the end experience salvation. Rather he believed that by the death of Christ the latter "procured this Grace and Favour with God for all Men without exception, viz. that they should receive from Him sufficient strength and means, or be enabled by Him, to Repent, and to beleeve. . . ." The grace of God was not to be restricted to any "determinite number of men," for that grace was "so free, rich, and abounding towards man-kind, that he seriously intends the salvation of all men".[48] The Arminian preacher could therefore stand before any audience and proclaim his message, secure in the belief that any individual was capable of accepting the offer of grace. For him it was not a case of preaching in order for God to use that medium to call forth his elect; rather preaching was the genuine extension of the offer of grace to all men.

Unlike Owen, Baxter, and John Goodwin, Bunyan did not devote any of his literary efforts to a discussion of the extent of the atonement. What he did say on the subject was fragmentary and slightly contradictory. On the one hand he wrote that Christ "by the grace of God tasted death for every man," and that he was exalted by God "for the sweet Savour that he smelled in his Blood, when he dyed for the Sins of the World". On the other hand, in the same work from which the first of the two preceding quotations was taken, he remarked that Christ

reconciled to God in the body of his Flesh as a common person, all, and every one of God's Elect. Christ, when he addressed himself to die, presented himself to the Justice of the Law, as a common Person; standing in the stead, place, and room of all that he undertook for [i.e., the elect]. . . .

The concept of a limited atonement was reflected elsewhere in his writings, as in his statement that "all the Elect did Mystically hang upon the Cross in Christ," and that "the Blood of Christ is sprinkled upon the Elect for the Justice of God to look on. . . ." Yet again, he wrote that Christ made satisfaction "for all Wrongs done, or to be done, by his Elect . . .," and that he "doth but petitionarily ask for his own, his purchased ones, those, for whom he died before, that they might be saved by his Blood".[49]

Bunyan did not doubt the sufficiency of Christ's death to save the whole world, but neither did Owen. In fact, most of Bunyan's statements on this subject are in harmony with Owen's position. Certainly he would not have agreed with John Goodwin. In spite of the occasional statements which he did make indicative of a general atonement it is not likely that he would have advocated a mediatory position, such as that of Baxter. The distinct majority of his statements on this subject indicate that he believed in a limited atonement. Yet the acerbity with which Owen advocated that doctrine was not acceptable to Bunyan, who was at least willing to tolerate a more liberal view. Christ "as a Propitiation," he wrote, was "not ours only, but also for the Sins of the whole World; to be sure, for the Elect throughout the World, and they that will extend it further, let them."[50]

On the question of the atonement in general, Bunyan's doctrine was quite compatible with the strict Calvinism of the period, such as that of John Owen and Thomas Goodwin. Increasing differences become apparent when his doctrine is compared with the moderate Calvinism of Baxter and the Arminianism of John Goodwin. With the Quaker position he was also at variance. His concept of satisfaction was learned neither from Luther nor from Arthur Dent, not necessarily because it was foreign to their thought, but rather because they did not discuss it in the works which Bunyan read. Likewise, the little which could be gleaned from Bayly's *Practise of Pietie*—and indeed, from the Bible itself—on the concept of satisfaction would hardly have provided Bunyan with the source material for his essentially Anselmic doctrine. Rather, it is more likely that he learned that doctrine from his Calvinist pastors, John Gifford and John Burton, and possibly from his ministerial friends such as John Owen. In any case, the work of Christ was one of Bunyan's principal topics in his

THE PILGRIM'S GOD

first five years of preaching, as he himself reported in his spiritual autobiography. It was a fitting subject of concern for the seventeenth century pilgrim, who believed that without Christ's work there would be no pilgrimage at all. All hope for security from divine wrath rested on the work of grace in the atonement.

Notes

1. XXII, pp. 106–107.
2. XLV, p. 1; Bayly, *The Practise of Pietie* (3rd ed.; 1613), pp. 60–61 (cf. pp. 26 and 61–62). Nowhere was Bunyan's discussion of the nature of God as extensive as that of Bayly in the latter work, which Bunyan might have been expected to follow.
3. See Richard L. Greaves, 'Luther's Doctrine of Grace', *Scottish Journal of Theology*, XVIII (December, 1965), 385–95.
4. Luther, *A Commentarie of Master Doctor Martin Luther upon the Epistle . . . to the Galathians* (1635), fol. 16 verso. Luther subsequently qualified this maxim by permitting such discussion in debates with Jews, Turks, Papists, and heretics. Cf. fol. 17.
5. XLV, p. 1.
6. VII, pp. 17–18; XIII, p. 23; XII, pp. 59–60.
7. *The Works of Thomas Goodwin, D.D.* (1681–1704), I, pt. 2, pp. 160–61 and IV, pt. 1, p. 11.
8. XLVI, p. 219.
9. Cf. John Owen, *Salus Electorum* (1648), p. 145; and James Ussher, *A Body of Divinitie* (1645), p. 70; and the contrary position of John Goodwin, *An Exposition of the Nineth Chapter of the Epistle to the Romans* (1653), pp. 157–58.
10. XII, p. 72; Baxter, *The Right Method* (1653), p. 44; XII, p. 38.
11. XXII, p. 51 (cf. Matt. iii. 10); XXXIV, p. 116 (cf. pp. 128–29 and XII, pp. 59 and 197); XI, pp. 63–64; XVIII, p. 137.
12. XII, p. 41 (cf. Bayly, *Pietie*, pp. 52–53).
13. Cf., e.g., T. Goodwin, *Works*, III, pt. 1, p. 598; and also Bayly, *Pietie*, p. 55.
14. XXXII, sect. 150; XII, p. 300; XXXVII, p. 152.
15. T. Goodwin, *Works*, I, pt. 2, p. 154. Cf. George Fox, *Journal* (Cambridge, 1952), pp. 11, 13; and Nuttall, *The Holy Spirit*, pp. 39–40.
16. XII, p. 215; LIII, p. 414.
17. LIII, p. 403 (cf. p. 411 and I John iv. 8); T. Goodwin, *Works*, I, pt. 2, p. 135 (cf. pp. 143, 271); *ibid.*, p. 142.

18. Bayly, *Pietie*, p. 52; Owen, *Salus Electorum*, p. 149; Ussher, *Body of Divinitie*, p. 65.
19. LIII, p. 414; Saltmarsh, *Free-Grace* (1645), fol. A4.
20. For the former position see Bayly, *Pietie*, p. 63; T. Goodwin, *Works*, IV, pt. 1, pp. 3, 42, 44; and Thomas Collier, *The Body of Divinity* (1674), pp. 14–16. For the latter position see Ussher, *Body of Divinitie*, p. 67; and Owen, *Christologia, or, a Declaration of . . . the Person of Christ* (1679), pp. 245–46.
21. XII, p. 327; XV, p. 26; LIV, p. 256; T. Goodwin, *Works*, I, pt. 2, p. 245. Owen, on the other hand, defined mercy (and grace) as the "Goodness, Kindness, and Benignity of God in Christ". *An Exposition on the Third, Fourth, and Fifth Chapters of . . . Hebrews* (1674), p. 323 (cf. p. 320).
22. Cf. Bayly, *Pietie*, pp. 52–53; Ussher, *Body of Divinitie*, p. 67; T. Goodwin, *Works*, IV, pt. 1, pp. 23, 37, 38; Dent, *The Plaine Mans Path-Way to Heauen* (1601), p. 408.
23. XLVI, p. 219. Cf. T. Goodwin, *Works*, I, pt. 3, pp. 64–65.
24. XLI, p. 39.
25. LVI, p. 559. Cf. T. Goodwin, *Works*, I, pt. 2, pp. 138, 257; Owen, *An Exposition of the Two First Chapters of . . . Hebrews* (1668), p. 215; Ussher, *Body of Divinitie*, p. 69; Bayly, *Pietie*, pp. 53–54; J. Goodwin, *The Remedie of Unreasonableness* (1650), p. 6; Tobias Crisp, *Christ Alone Exalted* (1690), IV, 26.
26. LIV, pp. 257, 256; XII, p. 118.
27. XXII, pp. 114–15; LVI, p. 562; XII, p. 118.
28. Saltmarsh, *Free-Grace*, p. 124; VII, p. 17; XLI, p. 35; XXXVI, p. 65.
29. XII, pp. 325, 193; LVI, p. 562; XV, pp. 9–10 (cf. Luke xxiv. 47); XXVI, p. [76].
30. XLII, p. 204; LVI, pp. 561–62 and XLV, p. 62; T. Goodwin, *Works*, III, pt. 3, p. 13 (cf. I, pt. 2, p. 150); Fowler, *The Design of Christianity* (1671), pp. 84–85; VIII, p. 30. Initially, Owen's position was that of T. Goodwin and Fowler (cf. *Salus Electorum*, p. 57), though in his *Diatriba de Justitia Divina* of 1653, he changed his mind and defended the absolute necessity of an atonement.
31. XXVI, p. [96]. Owen's definition of satisfaction as "a full compensation of the Creditour from the Debtor . . ." was similar. *Salus Electorum*, p. 137. T. Goodwin defined it as "a return of as much Glory [to God] as was lost. . . ." *Works*, III, pt. 3, p. 108.
32. XXVI, p. [52]; XII, p. 203 (cf. p. 72).

33. XLVI, p. 224; P[enn], *The Sandy Foundation Shaken* (1668), pp. 19–20, 16.
34. VIII, pp. 114ff.; Penn, *Sandy Foundation*, p. 16; Fowler, *Design*, p. 84; VIII, p. 30; XLIII, p. 398.
35. XXXVIII, p. 145; XXXVII, p. 214; B[urrough], *The True Faith* (1656), p. 26. For a scholarly examination of the Socinian movement, see H. J. McLachlan, *Socinianism in Seventeenth-Century England* (Oxford, 1951).
36. XII, p. 34. For the strict Calvinist position see Bayly, *Pietie*, p. 1009; Owen, *Salus Electorum*, pp. 141–42; Ussher, *Body of Divinitie*, pp. 170–71. For the moderate Calvinist position see Baxter, *Catholick Theologie* (1675), Bk. I, pt. 2, chaps. xlviii–xlix, lii. Cf. J. Goodwin, *Impvtatio Fidei* (1642), pt. 2, p. 33.
37. Baxter, *Catholick Theologie*, Bk. I, pt. 2, chap. xlvii. Cf. Baxter, *The Reasons of the Christian Religion* (1667), p. 407; J. Goodwin, *Impvtatio Fidei,* pt. 2, p. 33; and Fowler (?), *Dirt Wip't Off* (1672), p. 51.
38. XII, p. 191 (cf. XXVI, p. [52]). Cf. Owen, *Salus Electorum*, pp. 138, 142, 154; Ussher, *Body of Divinitie*, p. 171; T. Goodwin, *Works*, III, pt. 3, p. 16; Crisp, *Christ Exalted*, II, 275.
39. LIV, p. 260; XI, p. 99 (cf. XLVIII, p. 78); XXVI, pp. [59–60].
40. For the strict Calvinist position see Ussher, *Body of Divinitie*, p. 170; and Thomas Gouge, *The Principles of Christian Religion* (1675), p. 9. For the Arminian position see J. Goodwin, *Impvtatio Fidei*, pt. 2, pp. 9–10.
41. Denne, *Truth Outweighing Error* (1673), p. 14.
42. Cf. Baxter, *Catholick Theologie*, Bk. I, pt. 2, pp. 14, 21, and chap. xlix; and Fowler, *Dirt*, p. 52.
43. LVI, p. 569; XXXVII, pp. 188–89 (cf. XII, pp. 323–26).
44. XXVI, p. [83] (cf. XII, p. 191; XLVIII, p. 79); LIII, p. 417; XXVI, p. [84] (cf. pp. [63ff.]); Baxter, *Catholick Theologie*, Bk. I, pt. 2, p. 16 and chaps. xlii and xlv (cf. J. Goodwin, *Impvtatio Fidei*, pt. 2, p. 26).
45. XLI, p. 33 (cf. Owen, *Salus Electorum*, pp. 141, 163–64; Fowler, *Design*, pp. 84–85); T. Goodwin, *Works*, III, pt. 3, p. 73.
46. Owen, *Salus Electorum*, p. 102; *Theomachia Autexousiastike: or, a Display of Arminianisme* (1643), pp. 94, 93. For other statements of this position see, e.g., *Westminster Confession*, VIII, v; T. Goodwin, *Christ Set Forth* (1642), p. 269; John Tombes, *Anti-Paedobaptism: or the Third Part* (1657), p. 247; Saltmarsh, *Free-Grace*, pp. 202–203;

Vavasor Powell, *Christ and Moses Excellency* (1650), pp. 109ff.
47. Baxter, *Catholick Theologie,* Bk. I, pt. 2, chaps. xcviii, c.
48. J. Goodwin, *Redemption Redeemed* (1651), pp. 74, 433; J. Goodwin *et al., Eirenomachia. The Agreement & Distance of Brethren* (1652), p. 31. For other statements of the Arminian position see, e.g., Thomas Grantham, *Christianismus Primitivus* (1678), Bk. 2, pp. 48, 63–64; *An Orthodox [General Baptist] Creed* (1678), art. xviii, in *Confessions of Faith,* ed. E. B. Underhill (1854), pp. 138–39; Fox, *Journal,* ed. Norman Penney (Cambridge, 1911), I, 294; and Robert Barclay, *An Apology for the True Christian Divinity* (1678), pp. 71ff.
49. LIII, p. 418 (cf. Heb. ii. 9); VIII, p. 57; LIII, p. 417; VIII, p. 55 (cf. XLVIII, p. 79); XXVI, p. [15]; XLII, p. 95 (cf. p. 207); XLIII, p. 370 (cf. pp. 389–90, 397).
50. XLII, p. 69 (cf. I John ii. 2).

2 The Pilgrim's Call

THE ALLEGORICAL JOURNEY depicted by Bunyan in *The Pilgrim's Progress* had its counterpart not only in actual Christian living in the seventeenth century but also in contemporary theology. The Christian life was in reality a soteriological journey which commenced with the trek from the City of Destruction and continued through the wicket gate to the Palace Beautiful and ultimately to the final but glorious place of eternal dwelling with God. Bunyan had much to say about the theological aspects of this soteriological journey; what he said placed him quite firmly in the strict Calvinist tradition. What he said also was essentially representative of that which any Puritan or sectary in the seventeenth century would have heard from his own strict Calvinist minister on the subject of salvation.

Bunyan, unlike Luther, thought of salvation as much in terms of a process as an achieved fact and present possession of the believer. Simply considered, salvation involved the twofold aspect of justification and preservation. On the one hand, to be saved in the sense of being justified was "to be delivered from guilt of Sin that is by the Law, as it is the Ministration of Death and Condemnation; or, to be set free therefrom, before God". Salvation in this sense was a present possession of the believer. On the other hand, salvation in the sense of preservation was "a saving of us by preserving us, by delivering of us from all those hazards that we run betwixt our state of Justification, and our state of Glorification". When conceived of in this sense salvation could never be a present possession of the believer until he was resurrected at the culmination of his pilgrimage.[1]

Salvation was, for Bunyan, a more complex process, however, than merely justification and preservation. "To save, is a work of many steps, or to be as plain as possible, to save, is a work that hath its beginning before the World began, and shall not be compleated before it is ended." The steps which were involved in this process of salvation included election, calling, faith, repentance, justification, forgiveness, sanctification, and perseverance. Thomas Goodwin also distinguished between salvation as a present possession and a process. "Our Salvation is in God's Gift; and in Christ's personating of us and apprehending of us, it is perfect and compleat; though in our Persons, as in us, it is wrought by degrees." Goodwin could thus affirm that believers were saved in the present and yet speak of "the parts of Salvation and Works of God in us, which God carrieth on in us by degrees. . . ."[2]

For Bunyan salvation signified, as it had for Luther, fundamentally escape from the awesome wrath of God. The emphasis of both Luther and Bunyan was on salvation *from* something, whereas most Calvinists, while acknowledging that the elect were saved from sin and divine wrath, nevertheless stressed salvation *to* something, namely, the holy life of a regenerated man.[3] Bunyan, of course, certainly did not ignore the holy life, but in his discussions of salvation there was a definite tendency for him to be concerned with the believer's freedom from divine punishment. Undoubtedly his personal religious experience was responsible for this tendency. The resulting difference in emphasis was a partial cause of the bitter controversy between Bunyan and Edward Fowler. The theme of Fowler's treatise on *The Design of Christianity* was precisely that the purpose of Christ's life and death was "to make men in all respects Vertuous and Holy . . .," whereas for Bunyan the purpose was to appease divine justice and displeasure, and to save men from the curse of God.[4]

Salvation for Bunyan meant "eternal preservation and security" as well as "fortification and safety" from the wrath of an angry God. Experience had taught him that "he, that is astonished with, and that trembleth at the wrath of God, he knows best what it is to be saved. . . ." Yet salvation was more than escape from divine wrath, hence Bunyan, generally using biblical terminology, described it as redemption or deliverance from sin, death, the devil, hell, the law, and the human "state of thraldom and misery". The end or purpose of this salvation was man's enjoyment of God and God's everlasting glorification by those whom he had saved.[5]

The Role of Predestination: Election

THO a River, in the Streams of it, is common, yet a River, as it passes thorow a Country or Province, will chuse its own way. 'Twill run in the Valleys, in the Plains, not over Steeples and Hills. 'Twill also fetch its compasses and circuits; 'twill go about and reach hither and thither; and according to its courses, 'twill miss, by its turnings, what Places, and People it lists; yet it is common, for that it lies open; yet it is common for all the Beasts of the Field.[6]

The grace of God was likened by Bunyan to such a river, flowing where and when it would, selecting or rejecting whomever it wished. The purposeful meandering of the river was for Bunyan an illustration in nature of the theological concept of predestination, the basis of which was the sovereign grace of God.

The primacy of predestination in the soteriological journey was indicated by Bunyan when he made election and reprobation respectively the first steps on his "map" depicting the order and causes of salvation and damnation.[7] Between the eternal act of predestination (election and reprobation) and the temporal acts of effectual calling and the legal conviction of sin the covenant scheme was inserted into the plan of salvation and damnation. Election was thus the foundation of the covenant of grace, and reprobation the foundation of the covenant of works. Consequently predestination was the focal point of all that followed in the salvation process. Predestination itself, however, as the illustration of the meandering river indicated, was grounded in divine grace, which may rightly be considered the key to Bunyan's thought.

Election was defined by Bunyan as the free choice or decree of God to grant to certain men eternal life. This was a typically Calvinist definition, and was quite distinct from the innocuous Arminian definition of election: "Whosoever beleeveth, shall be saved. . . ." The Quakers were Arminian in their concept of predestination, as George Fox's idea of election indicates: "Soe all y^t beleives in ye light of Christ as hee commands are in ye election & setts under ye grace of Gods teachinge y^t bringes there salvation. . . ." For the Arminian, faith brought election; for the Calvinist election brought faith.[8]

According to Bunyan election occurred prior to the actual creation of man, God having foreseen that man would sin and thus merit eternal damnation. Consequently election was subsequent to God's foreknowledge of the fall, but prior to the fall itself. Bunyan was thus an infralapsarian. The Arminians, on the other hand, made election subsequent to and dependent on both God's foreknowledge of the fall *and* his foreknowledge of an individual's faith. Simultaneously the Arminians distinguished between the decree of election, which antedated the creation of man, and the actual election of individual persons, who were chosen only *after* they had professed faith in God. Bunyan, however, was thoroughly Calvinist in contending that "this Decree, Choice or Election, was before the Foundation of the World; and so before the Elect themselves, had Being in themselves. . . ."[9] Yet Bunyan was also careful to emphasise that it was the salvation of some of *fallen* mankind which God determined. Bunyan believed that God in his grace elected man because he knew that man would fall and be damned, not that God in his sovereignty elected man and *then* either decreed or permitted the fall in order to glorify his love and justice in election and reprobation (which was the supralapsarian position).

Such salvation by election was always considered by Bunyan within the framework of grace: election "hangeth upon the . . . Hinge [of] . . . the Grace of God. . . ." Election was "founded in

Grace", and it was by this grace that election "layeth hold of Men. . . ." "The Father, by his Grace hath bound up them that shall go to Heaven in an eternal Decree of Election . . ." and apart from this election of grace there was no salvation. Grace was even personalised by Bunyan in order to dramatise its importance for election: "'Tis Grace that chooses . . .;" "only so many, are brought home to God, as Grace is pleased to bring home to him."[10]

Election was a matter relating not only to grace, but also to the divine will and purpose. In the salvation of a sinner grace worked in accordance with the purpose of God. "God in thus saving, may be said to save us, by determining to make those means effectual for the blessed compleating of our Salvation: And hence we are said, to be chosen in Christ to Salvation. . . ." Underlying this purpose or determination on the part of God to make the means of salvation effectual to the elect was his unchangeable will which determined that election would be both free and permanent. It was, argued Bunyan, the "Prerogative Royal" of God to "chuse and refuse at pleasure" whomever he wished according to his own good pleasure.[11] Both the Calvinists and the Arminians stressed this sovereignty or pleasure of God in election. But whereas the Calvinists used this sovereignty to vindicate the divine choice of individuals without respect to any such conditions as faith and repentance, the Arminians used the concept of sovereignty to defend God's prerogative to elect according to "the rule of Faith. . . ."[12]

With the indignation of the staunchest Calvinist Bunyan criticised Edward Fowler for having decried "the Irrespectiveness of God's Decrees. . . ." To question election, and by this Bunyan meant election as it was taught by the Calvinists, was tantamount to rejecting the omniscience, omnipotence, and will of God; to taking away God's liberty with his creation; and to making salvation depend upon works rather than grace.[13] Election was thus used by Bunyan to defend and exemplify both the sovereignty of God and the freeness of grace. In contrast, however, to much of contemporary Calvinism, which developed election and sovereignty primarily against a background of philosophical determinism,[14] Bunyan's doctrine of election was a natural outgrowth of his experience of the primacy of God in salvation—an experience which he found paralleled in the writings of Paul and Luther. That experience had led them as well to develop a doctrine of divine election.[15]

The conviction that the divine decree of election involved specific sinners rather than a general proposition such as that stated in John iii. 16, was held by Bunyan early in his religious experience. Had he believed that there was nothing more to election than the Arminian contention that whoever believed was consequently elected and would be saved, there would not have been the agonising struggles recorded in *Grace Abounding* concerning the question, "How can you tell you are Elected?" Election did not mean the predestination of those who would believe to eternal life, but rather the choice of certain individuals before the creation of the world who alone would be given the necessary ability to believe.[16]

The covenant which Bunyan believed was established between the Father and the Son involved only this predetermined number of elect souls. Bunyan described these souls as those "that the Father hath given to Christ to keep them; those, that Christ hath promised Eternal Life unto, those to whom he hath given his Word, and that he will have with him in his Kingdom to behold his Glory. . . ." Election meant that on the part of God there was "distinguishing love" for only some men. This distinguishing love or electing grace was that which was set forth in terms of a covenant (or promise) in Jer. xxxii. 38–40.

> . . . The grace of God
> Takes hold on but a few,

a predetermined number sufficient to take the place of the fallen angels. For those excluded from these few selected by God's distinguishing love there was no provision of effectual grace. "There was Grace for Lot, but none for his Wife . . .", for Jacob but not for Esau, for David but not for Saul, for Peter but not for Judas. The elect—and only the elect—were those appointed to believe. Effectual grace was reserved for them.[17]

Election was so predominantly the gracious and sovereign act of God that it in no way, said Bunyan, took into consideration an individual's eventual faith, goodness, or works, as the Arminians contended.[18] Precisely the opposite was true, for it was as a *result* of their election that sinners were given the faith to believe and the graces that accompanied their salvation. For those fortunate enough to be among these select few, salvation was virtually assured, for there was no "impediment attending the Election of God, that can hinder their Conversion, and eternal Salvation". The conclusion that "all the sins they commit, and all the judgments they deserve, cannot drive them out of the World before Conversion," must have been derived by Bunyan at least in part from his providential preservation on those occasions in his life when he narrowly escaped death.[19]

The finality of election was assured, Bunyan affirmed, by its being as eternal as God himself, absolute rather than conditional, and grounded in divine foreknowledge. "The Eternal Inheritance is, by a Covenant of free and unchangeable Grace, made over to those thus chosen." That election was final and unchangeable, however, did not at all mean a denial or a lessening of the importance of the ordained means of salvation, "but rather putteth a Necessity upon the Use and Effect thereof; because they are chosen to be brought to Heaven that way: that is by the Faith of Jesus Christ, which is the end of effectual calling". The purpose of God in decreeing this final and unchangeable election was, said Bunyan, the manifestation of his glory, love, and power.[20]

Having heard this doctrine preached from the pulpit, the one question of supreme importance for the man in the pew could not help but be, "How can you tell you are Elected?" Mere natural light was said to be insufficient to attain this knowledge. Yet the man who was sincerely seeking Christ purportedly already had some evidence of his election, for "coming to Christ, is by vertue of the gift, promise, and drawing of the Father; but thou art a coming, therefore God hath given thee, promised thee, and is drawing thee to Jesus Christ". It was necessary first to prove one's calling before a man was able to know with certainty that he had been elected.

Thou shalt not know thy election in the first place, but in the second. That is to say, thou must first get acquaintance with God in Christ, which doth come by thy giving credit to his promises, and records which he hath given of Jesus Christ, his blood and righteousness, together with the rest of his merits.

That is, before thou canst know whether thou art elected, thou must believe in Jesus Christ so really, that thy faith laying hold of . . . Christ, even so, that there shall be life begotten in thy soul by the same.

Ultimate assurance of election was dependent on the Spirit's testimony of the personal forgiveness of sins and the resulting realisation of God's goodness.[21]

The Role of Predestination: Reprobation

THE logical corollary of Bunyan's Calvinist doctrine of election was the assertion of divine reprobation. In his statement of this doctrine Bunyan adhered closely to such biblical proof as could be adduced for its support rather than appealing to philosophically-based theological arguments.[22] The one possible exception was his belief that God

is a free agent to do what he pleaseth, and may if he please refuse to give any thing, or if he gives something, why may he not give what he pleases also? He may give special grace to one, and that which is not so to another. . . . He may suffer some to fall away, and keep others by his power, through faith unto salvation.

Even this statement, however, was based on a living experience of God's sovereignty and the testimony to that sovereignty recorded in the Bible, not on an abstract theological argument. Bunyan was personally convinced that there could be no thought of denying God's "Prerogative Royal, without prejudice to them that are damned, [to] chuse and refuse at pleasure. . . ."[23]

Reprobation was explained in three basic ways by the men of

56

the seventeenth century. Writers such as Owen, Ussher, and Dent conceived of reprobation as a positive decree of rejection by God. Somewhat mitigated was the concept of reprobation as non-election, which was held by men such as Thomas Goodwin, Baxter, and Vavasor Powell. The third concept of reprobation was that advocated by the Arminians, who explained it in this manner: "when God, upon mens neglect, refusall, or abuse of the meanes of grace vouchsafed unto them, shall withdraw these meanes to such a degree, that they fall to open prophanesse [*sic*], loosenesse, &c. he is now said to have reprobated them, not because he had at any time before passed an act of Reprobation against them, which was now put in execution. . . ." The Quakers manifested Arminian tendencies, with Fox, for example, rejecting the notion that men were ordained for hell. The Quaker leader instead asserted that only "such as turnes this grace Into wantonesse are in ye reprobation. . . ."[24]

Bunyan chose to define reprobation primarily in terms of non-election, or the leaving of sinners by God "in their sins to perish by his judgments. . . ." Yet in time God was said to act positively by blinding the eyes and hardening the heart of the reprobate so that he "cannot repent, nor be profited by the means of Grace. . . ." Referring at once to the rich man mentioned in Luke xvi and to Mr. Badman, Bunyan observed that God "had a mind to damn him for his sins, and therefore would not let him see nor have an heart to repent for them, lest he should convert, and his damnation, which God had appointed, should be frustrate. . . ." For the reprobate who had become one of the "great Transgressors" there was no possibility of saving grace, for he "hath received in his Mind the stroke of the Judgment of God, and . . . is denied all Means of Saving and Sanctifying Grace. . . ." Even Owen was not as extreme as Bunyan in this regard, for the former believed that none were destitute of the assistance of divine grace except those who, by a free act of their wills, rejected it. The Arminians, of course, steadfastly insisted that "the reason of any mans perishing [cannot] be ascribed unto God, or to any denial, or withholding of Grace by him. . . ."[25]

Although reprobation was at least a negative act of God, the responsibility for eternal damnation was, according to Bunyan, entirely man's. It was not because of providence or non-election that men were damned, but because of their sin—and "they sinned, not because God put any weakness into their Souls, but because they gave way, and that wilfully, knowingly, and desperately, to Satan. . . ." The reprobate had been besought by God to accept his grace; it was their obstinate refusal to do so which was the cause of their eternal punishment. Reprobation itself, however, as distinct from damnation, was caused not by sin, but by the fact that "only so many, are brought home to God, as Grace is pleased to bring home to him". Those who were not elected by grace were consequently reprobated. There was no other alternative.[26]

Even as the corollary to the doctrine of election is the doctrine of reprobation, so the corollary to the question about personal assurance of that election is the query concerning the marks of the reprobate.[27] That which distinguished the elect from the reprobate was, Bunyan indicated, the possession of the Spirit; consequently a mark of the reprobate was said to be the taunting of the Spirit and dallying with God. Another mark was procrastination, for it was "the hard hap of the Reprobate to do all things too late; to be sensible of his want of Grace too late; to be sorry for Sin too late; to seek Repentance too late; to ask for Mercy, and to desire to go to Glory, too late". The one infallible mark of reprobation was, obviously, the sin of final impenitence.[28]

The Problem of Free Will

TO say that certain specific persons had been elected before their birth to salvation, and that these, and these alone, would be infallibly saved, and that the rest of mankind were reprobates with no possibility of such salvation, was to imply some divine control over the human will. Thus John Owen wrote that "the certaintie of divers promises and threatnings of Almightie God, dependeth upon his powerfull determining, and turning the wils and hearts of men which way he pleaseth. . . ." A Calvinist, believing in election and reprobation, could adopt one of two positions with regard to human will: he could argue either that man's will was in no way free to choose God (the strict Calvinist position), or that his will could cooperate with divine grace in making that choice (the moderate Calvinist position). There could, however, be no question of accepting the Arminian contention that the wills of men were free "to determine themselves, or make their elections [to God or to sin] freely", even with the added qualification that for the will to choose God without the assistance of his grace was impossible.[29]

Bunyan did not underestimate the importance of the will, which he regarded as the "chief seat of the heart" and the "chief and great faculty of the soul. . . . The will, which way that goes, all goes: If it be to Heaven or Hell". The will determined the relationship of the whole man to God: "Man, when his will is alienate from God, is reckoned rebellious throughout, . . . for the will is the principal faculty of the soul as to obedience. . . ." Although he attributed much significance to the will, Bunyan was careful to restrict severely its freedom, opposing anything which "savours too much of a Tang of Free-will, or of the sufficiency of our understanding, and intrencheth too hard on the Glory of the Holy Ghost. . . ." "I am not," he stated unequivocally, "a Free Willer, I do abhor it. . . ." Bunyan had read and faithfully heeded Luther's exhortation to "cast under our feet, and utterly abhorre all the power of freewill . . . as a most filthy defiled cloath, and as the most dangerous poison of the devill". In rejecting any notion of free will which would detract from the graciousness and sovereignty of God in salvation, Bunyan spoke more from a soteriological concern and in a soteriological context (as did Luther) than from the scholastic principles of a philosophical-theological system (as did Owen).[30]

There was a sense in which man did have free will, that is, to the extent that he could, as Bunyan phrased it, "do, and chuse to do, either that which by all men is counted base, or that which by some is counted good, though he is not . . . capable of doing any thing that may please his God". Such a position was

commonly accepted by most seventeenth century writers, including John Goodwin, who agreed with the Calvinists that no man
by nature had the power or disposition to do anything that was
spiritually good. Bunyan himself went so far as to admit that man
had both the will and power to pursue his own salvation, but he
rejected any notion of man being able to pursue salvation in a
way acceptable to God. The crucial point was that "the Soul
where grace is wanting, is not at liberty to act simply, but is
byassed by the power of sin. . . ." Man's will was not so free that
he could will to be saved "God's way, to wit, by Jesus Christ,
before . . . the day of God's power comes upon him".[31]

The idea (as expressed by Fowler) that men had the ability to
"cooperate with the grace of God or . . . do any thing towards
their own salvation . . ." as the result of the principle of freedom
with which they were endued was totally unacceptable to Bunyan.
Instead, because of their nature men had to be *made* willing by
divine grace to believe in God. According to Bunyan, God was
"forced . . . to whip souls to Jesus Christ. . . ." To do this God
first implanted a desire for salvation and then granted the necessary power "to pursue thy Will in the matters of thy Salvation.
. . ." The reprobate could not object that divine grace did not
work in such a manner in their wills, for "God did not determine
to bring them to Heaven against their hearts and wills, and the
love that they had to their sins. . . ."[32]

In spite of the fact that man himself could not will to believe in
God, Bunyan nevertheless repeatedly exhorted his readers to
"take heed, Sirs, break off your sins . . ." and "come to God in
the Name of the Son . . . and beg faith of him. . . ." Such exhorta-
tions were based on the idea that—to return to the illustration of
the meandering river—"the Waters [of grace] are common, but
you must come to them . . . where they are, or you will be nothing
the better for them". Indeed, it was the reprobates' refusal of this
grace—even though they did not have the free will to accept it—
that was the cause of their damnation. The paradoxical nature of
Bunyan's entire handling of man's will and God's grace was
summed up in one exhortation: "Get thy Will tipt with the

Heavenly Grace, and resolution against all discourag[e]ments, and then thou goest full speed for Heaven. . . ."[33]

The Divine Call

NOR can a man his Soul with Grace inspire,
More than can Candles set themselves on fire.

The Egg when laid, by Warmth is made a Chicken;
And Christ, by Grace, those dead in sin doth quicken.

These pieces of doggerel by Bunyan underscore his basic conviction that the initiative in the salvation of the pilgrim was wholly God's. For Bunyan, all men—the elect included— were spiritually dead until the Spirit entered "into them; until they shall drink it in by vehement thirst as the parched Ground drinks in the Rain". There could be no rain, no grace, unless God first sought the sinner. This initiative which he took in procuring the salvation of his elect was his act of calling.[34]

Calling, which in biblical language was expressed by such terms as quickening, awakening, illuminating, and the bringing forth from darkness into light,[35] had a threefold aspect in Bunyan's thought. There was first a personal realisation of the evil of sin and unbelief, as well as an awareness of being without Christ and hope. Second, there was a revelation of a world to come, of resurrection and judgement, and of salvation and future glory. Finally, there was a promise of complete sanctification. This calling was the result of election—of being ordained to eternal life; it was the "Fruit of electing Love". The elect were called on the basis of the covenant of grace, particularly as it was established between the Father and the Son. The means of this calling was the word of God, "for by the Word that calleth us, is Jesus Christ held forth to us; and offered to be our Righteousness. . . ."[36]

Calling was through and through a matter of grace. Grace itself, in fact, was said to do the calling. Furthermore, in order to make calling effectual "all manner of Grace" had to be given to the elect, and this was possible only because Christ "positively determineth to put forth a sufficiency of all Grace that shall Effectually perform this promise".[37]

To speak of an effectual call and the sufficiency of grace provided for the elect was to raise one of the more controversial religious questions of the seventeenth century: could calling, could the grace of God, be resisted? Mention has already been made of the fact that, according to Bunyan, man could not himself will to be saved God's way apart from the working of grace on his will. If, then, man was not free to choose salvation but had to be dependent on divine grace, was he free to reject that grace if it was offered to him? The Calvinist position was that effectual calling (or grace) could not be resisted. In the representative words of Owen,

> the effectuall grace which God useth in the great works of our conversion, by reason of its owne nature, being also the instrument of, and God's intention for that purpose, doth surely produce the effect intended; without successefull resistance, and solely, without any considerable cooperation of our owne wils, untill they are prepared and changed by that very grace.[38]

The Arminians conceded that grace was irresistible only to the extent that all men received a sufficiency of means by which it was possible for them to be saved. Apart from this, however, an Arminian did not believe that God would constrain a man by his grace to have faith.[39]

Bunyan's position was that effectual calling could not be resisted. Such calling he likened to the call of Jesus that had raised Lazarus from the dead: "A Word attended with an Arm that was omnipotent", and a word that "outwent all Opposition. . . ." Temporary refusal might be possible, but, as Captain Judgement warned Mansoul in *The Holy War*, man could not long resist the conquering power of a sovereign God. "Shall God speak to mans soul? and shall not man believe? . . . It cannot be." The Vocation-doubter in *The Holy War* was condemned for rejecting the existence of "any such thing as a distinct and powerful call of God to Mansoul; otherwise than by the general voice of the Word, nor by that neither otherwise than as it exhorted them to forbear evil, and to do that which is good, and in so doing a promise of happiness is annexed". Bunyan's condemnation of the Vocation-doubter was in reality a condemnation of the Arminian concept of calling. Contrary to such a position, Bunyan affirmed the Calvinist belief that those who were personally and effectually called could not "stand off from Him, nor any longer [hold] out against Him, to whom he Reveals the Glory of his Grace". Effectual calling, then, meant irresistible grace. Yet not all men were called in this manner.[40]

For Bunyan, as for other Calvinists, there was also a type of calling which was not effectual, or in other words, a calling which man could refuse. Referring to Prov. i. 24–26, he noted that there were those who, having been called by God, refused that call and "despised the offer of his Grace. . . ." The penalty for this refusal was eternal damnation, but the condemned sinner could not help but admit that

The fault was mine, his Grace I did refuse . . .

Illustrating this idea for children, Bunyan pictured a child attempting to persuade a little bird to come to him for protection, only to discover that

. . . lo, behold, the Bird is gone;
These Charmings would not make her yield:
The Child's left at the Bush alone,
The Bird flies yonder o'er the Field.

The "comparison" which he wished to make was that

The Bird in that she takes her Wing,
To speed her from him after all:
Shews us, vain Man loves any thing,
Much better than the Heav'nly Call.[41]

That which made calling effectual was the power with which the Spirit accompanied the word of God, for apart from that power men neither could nor would hear and believe. It was the work of spiritual illumination upon the sinner's understanding which made him willing to accept the offer of grace. "Now when this living Water", this grace of the Holy Spirit, "is received, it takes up its Seat in the Heart, whence it spreads it self to the awakening of all the Powers of the Soul". Bunyan thus provided another illustration of Perry Miller's sapient observation that "when conversion was described in the vocabulary of psychology it became in effect a realignment of twisted pulleys and tangled ropes, permitting the blocks once more to turn freely and the tackle to run smoothly, in accordance with the first plan of the rigging". Bunyan also likened calling to one phase of animal husbandry: as a hen sits on her eggs until they are hatched, so the Spirit "sitteth and broodeth upon the Powers of the Soul . . ." until they are awakened to a true understanding of both spiritual and natural things. Then followed the conviction and confession of sin and the fear of divine judgement. It was not the fear of judgement alone, however, which persuaded a man to believe. Bunyan was careful to point out that it was not "the overheavy Load of Sin, but the Discovery of Mercy; not the Roaring of the Devil, but the Drawing of the Father, that makes a Man come to Jesus Christ: I my self know all these Things". On the basis of his own experience, he urged his readers to prove the reality of their own calling by the word of God, warning them that those who were uncertain of their calling could not comfortably hope for eternal life.[42]

NOTES

1. XLIII, p. 373.
2. LVI, p. 555; T. Goodwin, *Works*, I, pt. 2, pp. 217, 201, 279.
3. Cf. *A Commentarie of Master Doctor Martin Luther upon the Epistle . . . to the Galathians* (1635), fols. 20 *verso*–21; T. Goodwin, *Works*, I, pt. 1, p. 310, and pt. 2, p. 279; Owen, *Display of Arminianisme*, pp. 149–50; and Baxter, *A Treatise of Conversion* (1657), pp. 8, 11.
4. Fowler, *Design*, p. 68; VIII, pp. 8, 80.

5. XX, pp. 61–62; LVI, p. 554; XII, p. 122; XXVI, p. [97]; XXXVIII, p. 3.
6. XLI, p. 19. In another illustration of predestination T. Goodwin also stressed the passivity of man, and noted as well the apparent, though not actual, role of chance: "You have Heaven cast upon you (you that are Believers) as it were by lot. Poor Souls, you come hither to Church, and here you put your selves upon God's Lottery, and you do well. What is the reason, that a poor Servant goeth away with Christ in her heart? She hath a Draw for it, and she draweth Eternal life, it is cast upon her. . . . God had predestinated them, yet it is carried so as if it came to them by lot. . . ." *Works*, I, pt. 1, pp. 177–78.
7. LV.
8. LVI, p. 503; LVII, Vol. II, 52; Owen, *Display of Arminianisme*, p. 51; Ussher, *Body of Divinitie*, p. 91; J. Goodwin, *et al.*, *Agreement*, pp. 2–3; Fox, *Journal* (1911 ed.), I, 294–95.
9. LVII, Vol. II, 52
10. VIII, p. 75; LVII, Vol. II, 52; LVI, pp. 570, 560; LIV, p. 264; LVI, p. 571.
11. LVI, p. 555 (cf. Eph i. 3–4); XXXIV, p. 167; LVI, p. 559.
12. Bayly, *Pietie*, p. 172; Owen, *Display of Arminianisme*, pp. 51, 63–64; Ussher, *Body of Divinitie*, p. 91; *Westminster Confession*, III, v; J. Goodwin, *Romans*, pp. 105, 144.
13. Fowler, *Design*, p. 262; XXII, p. 381.
14. Cf., e.g., *Westminster Confession*, III, i.
15. Cf. XVI, sects. 45–48; and also Acts ix. 3–16; Rom. ix. 1lff.; Eph. i. 3–11; and Luther, *Galathians*, fols. 37 *verso*–38.
16. XVI sect. 47; XLII, pp. 42–43. Cf. Owen, *Display of Arminianisme*, p. 8; and T. Goodwin, *Works*, I, pt. 2, pp. 135, 145–46.
17. VII, pp. 14–15 (cf. pp. 71, 167); XXXIX, p. 97; XXVII, p. 16; LVI, p. 572 (cf. Baxter, *Catholick Theologie*, Bk. I, pt. 1, chap. cdxv).
18. Denne, *Truth Outweighing Error*, pp. 22–25, 31–32; J. Goodwin, *Romans*, pp. 132–33, 135, 165.
19. LVII, Vol. II, 53; LVI, p. 555; XVII, sects. 12–13.
20. XLII, pp. 42–43; LVII, Vol. II, 53.
21. XVI, sect. 47; VII, p. 217; XII, p. 373.
22. On the problem of the authorship of *Reprobation Asserted* [c. 1674], which would necessitate a modification of this statement if Bunyan were the author, see Richard L. Greaves, "John Bunyan

and the Authorship of *Reprobation Asserted*," *The Baptist Quarterly*, XXI (July, 1965).

23. XXI, pp. 55–56; XXXIV, p. 167 (cf. Bayly, *Pietie*, p. 1011).

24. Owen, *Salus Electorum*, p. 114; Ussher, *Body of Divinitie*, p. 92; Dent, *Path-Way*, p. 298; T. Goodwin, *Works*, II, pt. 4, pp. 195–96; Baxter, *Catholick Theologie*, Bk. I, pt. 1, chaps. cdlvii–cdlix, cdlxiv, dclxviii; Powell, *Christ and Moses*, pp. 14–15; J. Goodwin, *Redemption Redeemed*, p. 62; Fox, *Journal* (1911 ed.), I, 294, 295.

25. XXI, p. 87; II, p. 71 (cf. Rom. xi. 10); XXV, p. 337; XLV, p. 32; Owen, *A Treatise of the Dominion of Sin and Grace* (1688), p. 14; J. Goodwin, *et al.*, *Agreement*, p. 46.

26. XXXIV, p. 168; LVI, p. 571.

27. A detailed picture of the reprobate's life, illustrating these marks, was painted by Bunyan in *The Life and Death of Mr. Badman* (1680).

28. XXXVII, fols. C5–C5 *verso*; XXIV, p. 108; II, pp. 28–29.

29. Owen, *Display of Arminianisme*, p. 36; J. Goodwin, *Redemption Redeemed*, p. 53.

30. XXXIX, pp. 223, 220–21; LIX, Vol. II, 106; LVIII, Vol. II, 837–38; Luther, *Galathians*, fol. 23 *verso*. In the Episcopal Returns for 1669 there was listed a group of "about 40" in Sundon, Beds., who were described as "Quakers" and "Freewill[rs]". A similar group was recorded in Milford, Hants. See *Original Records*, ed. Turner, I, 67, 142. The term could also, of course, refer to an Arminian.

31. XI, p. 81; J. Goodwin, *et al.*, *Agreement*, p. 57; XVIII, p. 31 (cf. Dent, *Path-Way*, pp. 6–7); LIII, p. 426.

32. Fowler, *Design*, pp. 230, 173, 9; XII, p. 240; VII, pp. 295–96; XXXIV p. 167.

33. XXV. p. 324 (cf. pp. 286, 310); XXXVII, p. 175; XLI, p. 20; XIX, p. 44. *The Holy War* (1682) provides a graphic illustration of the role of the will in the process of conversion. Cf. especially pp. 25–27, 72–73, 92, 126, 137–38, 144–45, 164–65, 178, and 182–83.

34. III, pp. 14, 7; XLI, p. 71.

35. LVII, Vol. II, 53, referring to Eph. ii. 1–2; Heb. x. 32; and I Peter ii. 9.

36. LVII, Vol. II, 53–54.

37. VII, pp. 70, 31. Cf. Owen, *Display of Arminianisme*, p. 145; Baxter, *Catholick Theologie*, Bk. I, pt. 1, chap. cdl.

38. Owen, *Display of Arminianisme,* p. 145. Cf. *Westminster Confession,* X, i–ii; T. Goodwin, *Works,* I, pt. 1, p. 187; Baxter, *Catholick Theologie,* Bk. I, pt. 2, 2nd unnumbered page after p. 26.
39. J. Goodwin, *Remedie,* p. 7; *Agreement,* pp. 8, 32, 47; Denne, *Truth Outweighing Error,* pp. 22, 26–27.
40. LVII, Vol. II, 53 (referring to John xi. 43); XXII, p. 65; XLIII, p. 392; XXII, pp. 381–82; VII, p. 101.
41. I, p. 212; XXXII, sect. 179; III, pp. 41–42.
42. XLI p. 71; Miller, *The New England Mind: The Seventeenth Century* (New York, 1939), p. 280; XLI, p. 72; VII, pp. 225–26.

3 The Pilgrim's Response

THE INITIATIVE IN SALVATION was God's, but once a man had been elected and called he had to respond. Without grace there could be no response, for man himself lacked the ability to believe and repent. Like other Calvinist preachers, Bunyan encouraged his hearers and readers to have faith and repent, all the while keeping in mind that even these acts were grounded in God's power and grace. Following faith and repentance came the divine reply of justification, forgiveness, and the life-long process of sanctification. The journey of salvation continued, with the pilgrim persevering through grace until the triumphal culmination of his trek in resurrection.

The Response of Faith

THE Lord Secretary took him [Captain Credence], and . . . said, I have made thee the Lords Lieutenant over all the forces in Mansoul; so that from this day forward, all men in Mansoul shall be at thy word, and thou shalt be he that shall lead in, and that shalt lead out Mansoul. Thou shalt therefore manage according to thy place, the war for thy Prince, and for the Town of Mansoul, against the force and power of Diabolus, and at thy command shall the rest of the Captains be.[1]

The call of Shaddai had been proclaimed to Mansoul; Mount Gracious and Mount Justice had been "cast up against" Mansoul by the troops of Emmanuel; the town had been conquered; and Captain Credence, whose colour-bearer was Mr. Promise, had been given command of Emmanuel's forces in Mansoul. Faith was thus of great importance in the salvation of the sinner, particularly once divine grace had made him willing to accept the call of God. From this point on, faith and grace become in Bunyan's thought the inseparable foundation upon which succeeding steps in the soteriological journey are based.

Faith, according to Bunyan, could not be divorced from grace, for it was grace which made faith possible both in its first inception and in its continued maintenance. Natural man was incapable of faith by himself, hence the objection, "I cannot believe in Christ," was to be met with the firm reply, "God hath promised to make thee believe". Faith had to be planted in man's heart, or, from a slightly different perspective, man had to be "implanted into the Faith of Christ . . .," a work which was accomplished by divine grace, as all Bunyan's contemporaries testified.

> Thus did I fit you then with Faith and Love,
> When you among your enemies did live. . . .

Faith was the gift of God (Eph. ii. 8), "not a qualification arising from the stock of nature. . . ." Captain Credence, it must be remembered, was not a resident of Mansoul but one of Emmanuel's officers. Faith was to be the result of "Gods operation"; consequently man believed "according to the working of his mighty Power. . . ." Faith's continuing dependence on God was indicated by God's being the source of its "nourishment, and supplies". Such faith was not indiscriminately given by God, but was granted to the elect alone.[2]

Although the Arminians agreed with Calvinists such as Bunyan on the necessity of divine grace to enable men to believe, they made the important qualification that all men were granted sufficient grace to enable them to believe if they so chose. The moderate Calvinists agreed with the Arminians in believing that

God provided sufficient grace to make it possible for any man to have faith, but they also noted that only those actually predestined to salvation did believe.[3]

The actual implantation of faith in the elect was attributed by Bunyan to the power of the Spirit. Faith was "wrought in the heart by an invisible operation of the Spirit, revealing the certainty of the satisfaction of the merits of Christ to the soul in a more glorious way, both for certainty and for durablenesse, both as to the promise and the constancy of it. . . ." Unless the Spirit worked in this manner there was no possibility of believing, for faith was not "to be found with any but those, in whom the Spirit of God by mighty Power doth work it; all others being fearful and incredulous, dare not venture their Souls and Eternity upon it", but trust to their own works. Having said this, however, Bunyan acknowledged that there was a type of faith which was not saving faith. Hence all those who professed to believe did not necessarily have the saving faith which only the Spirit through grace could implant in them.[4]

To define saving faith was no easy matter for one whose experience of conversion and the Christian life was a continuing tension between emotional experience and the rigid orthodox tenets of scholastic Calvinism. Something so spiritual in its nature and practical in its consequences, something which could only be ascribed to God's working in man and yet something which man was exhorted to have and exercise, perhaps no man could be expected to define adequately, given the imperfections and limitations of even the saintliest of the saints. For Bunyan faith was essentially

a principle of Life by which a Christian lives[,] . . . a principle of Motion by which it [i.e., the soul] walks towards Heaven in the Way of Holiness. . . . It is also a principle of strength, by which the soul opposeth its lust, the Devil and this World, and over-comes them. . . .

Faith meant action: a believer could not "sit still, Faith is forcible". Yet faith was not merely a matter of superactive ethics, but was also a response to God of the whole man, including the intellect. It was "a prevailing argument to the sinner, whereby he is fetched off from what he was, and constrained to bend and yeeld [*sic*] to what before it neither would nor could. . . ." Faith also involved a belief which embraced the gospel message. Faith, at least for Bunyan personally, meant not only belief in the gospel message itself, but also an element of "contemporaneousness" with the historical events recorded in that message: "Me thought I saw . . . the wonderful work of God in giving Jesus Christ to save us, from his conception and birth, even to his second coming to judgement: me thought I was as if I had seen him born, as if I had seen him grow up, as if I had seen him walk thorow this world, from the Cradle to his Cross. . . ." The element of contemporaneousness which Bunyan found in faith may have been inspired in him by Luther, who had written that "faith taketh hold of Christ, and hath him present, and holdeth him inclosed, as the ring doth the precious stone".[5]

Something as basic to salvation and the Christian life as faith was the subject of much literary endeavour in the sixteenth, and especially the seventeenth, centuries. Each man that attempted to define or describe such a personal reality could not escape the influence of his own experience of salvation and the Christian life. In his commentary on Galatians, Luther's basic concept of faith as an unfailing trust in Christ was evident in his definition of faith as "a certaine stedfast beholding, wch looketh upon nothing else but Christ. . . ." Baxter emphasised not so much the Christocentric as the anthropocentric (particularly the psychological) aspect of faith. For him faith was "the assent of the Intellect, . . . the consent of the Will, and . . . a practical affiance, trusting Christ as a Saviour. . . ." Thomas Goodwin's concept of faith as the resting of the heart upon Christ "nakedly and alone for life and salvation" was very much like that of Luther's. The same basic idea was reflected in the *Westminster Confession's* definition of faith as "Accepting, Receiving, and Resting upon Christ alone. . . ." John Saltmarsh laid special emphasis on the personal elements of confidence, persuasion, and trust, as did Dent and Bayly. Bunyan's view of faith as an all-embracing principle or source of the Christian life from its inception to its consummation had its closest parallel in Owen's definition of faith as "the Principle of Spiritual Light and Life in us".[6]

Faith, according to Bunyan, enabled the elect to "imbrace what by the word is set before them . . ." by illuminating the reality of the message. This was only possible if such faith was more than an historical faith derived from a study of biblical history, and was instead the result of "the cooperation of the Spirit with the Word". By carefully balancing the Spirit and the word (or Bible) Bunyan avoided both the excesses of hyper-intellectualism and traditionalism on his right, and the excesses of unmitigated spiritualism and mysticism on his left. The former tendency was approached by Baxter's intellectual and psychological definition of faith in terms of the faculties of the human soul. The latter tendency was exemplified in the Quaker conception of faith as belief and trust in "inward and immediate revelation" (*Deus loquens*). For Bunyan, however, faith could no more be divorced from the objective word than it could from the subjective working of the Spirit: "God mixeth it [i.e., faith] with the Word, when he absolutely intendeth the Salvation of the sinner. . . ." Bunyan would have agreed with Thomas Collier's insistence that "it must be a Word-Faith. . . ." It was this intimate association with the word which, for Bunyan, gave faith "an evidence of the certainty of what it believeth, . . . [for] that evidence is the infallible word of God".[7]

Faith was also associated by Bunyan with knowledge. The degree of faith which one attained was said to be directly dependent on one's knowledge of Christ. On the other hand, apart from faith there could be no true knowledge of God, for without such faith man "cannot but think of God amiss. . . ." It was faith which "brings God, Heaven, and Hell, to the soul, and maketh it duly consider of them all. . . ."[8]

Faith's most important work, according to Bunyan, was its role in the justification of the sinner. The righteousness of Christ had to be accepted by faith as that which justified the sinner before God, who imputed that righteousness to the one who had placed his trust in it for his salvation.

Now Faith hath it's eye upon two things, with respect to it's act of Justifying. First, it acknowledgeth that the Soul is a Sinner, and then that there is a sufficiency in the Righteousness of Christ, to Justifie it in the sight of God, though a Sinner.

Justifying faith, the object of which could be Christ alone, "laies hold on and applies, that which this Christ of God hath done, and is doing, and owns it as his own". Faith in itself merited nothing, but was divinely bestowed upon the elect as the instrument which enabled them to embrace the justifying righteousness of Christ. To have faith, then, was "to look to the perfect righteousness of Christ for life".[9]

The work of faith involved more, for Bunyan, than its role in justification. Having been justified, the sinner had to be assured by faith of the love of God, the forgiveness of sins, and his adoption as a son. As Luther had written: "With faith alwaies must be joyned a certaine assurance of Gods mercie. Now this assurance comprehendeth a faithfull trust of remission of sinnes for Christs sake". For Bunyan faith also brought an awareness to the justified sinner of the abundant grace which had been bestowed upon him in the initial steps of his soteriological journey and which continued to abide in him. It was also by faith that the heart had to be purified, sin vanquished, and the believer's life made holy. "A man is made good by Faith, and by that bringeth forth the Fruits that are acceptable to God. . . ." These fruits or works could be made acceptable only by faith—a faith that "worketh . . . by the Love of God. . . ." Faith was of supreme importance for the Christian life, for faith was "the onely instrument through the Spirit, that doth keep the soul in a comfortable frame, both to do and suffer for Christ; helps the soul to receive comfort from Christ, when it can get none from it self, beareth up the soul in its progress heaven-wards. . . ." By faith the believer could effectually challenge the power of sin, the law, death, and Satan. Finally, faith enabled the Christian to avoid both legal holiness—the "very deep Ditch" to the right of the path—and the temptation to turn divine grace into licentiousness—the "very dangerous Quagg" to the left of the path. Bunyan's attempt to maintain a balance between both objective and subjective extremes was here again made manifest.[10]

The dependence of faith on grace and the efficacious working of the Spirit did not prevent Bunyan from exhorting the sinner "to strive to pitch thy faith upon the Son of God. . . ." Although faith had to be implanted in man by God, the sinner could still "cry to God for faith . . ." and "come and buy such eye-salve of him that may make thee see". To do even this, however, was to glorify grace: "Believe in God's Mercy, through Jesus Christ, and so advance the Grace of God; I mean, venture heartily, venture confidently, for there is a sufficiency in the Grace of God."[11]

The Response of Repentance

BUT bring thou with thee a Certificate,
To shew thou seest thy self most desolate;
Writ by the Master, with Repentance seal'd,
To shew also that here thou wouldst be heal'd. . . .[12]

Repentance, like faith, was dependent on divine grace. It had to be bestowed on the sinner by God himself, for without the aid of grace man could not truly repent. On the other hand, once the Spirit had effectually worked on the sinner's mind, he could not help but repent. "For though a Man cannot appoint to himself when he will repent of his Sins, or when the Holy Ghost will work: yet he shall repent indeed; he shall do it, I say when He doth so work. . . ."[13] The primacy of God in the process of salvation was guarded by restricting the possibility of genuine repentance to the gracious and effectual working of the Spirit. This belief did not, however, discourage Bunyan from warning sinners not to delay their repentance.

Before there could be repentance there first had to be, on the part of the sinner, a true understanding of his sins, else, Bunyan wrote, he "cannot be affected with that grace that has laid hold on . . ." him. "There must be sound sence of sin, sound knowledge of God: Deep conviction of the certainty and terribleness of the day of Judgement, as also of the probability of obtaining Mercy." Not every "sight and sence" of sin produced true repentance, however, for a man could repent to the extent that he lived a righteous and religious life without having experienced the effectual grace which worked saving faith and repentance. God enabled the sinner to have a true awareness of his sins both by the light of the word and Spirit and by the temptations of the devil.[14]

Repentance itself, which was a result of effectual calling, was a complex act, involving several constituent parts. To repent was, first, to be sorry for and to be ashamed of one's sins, and consequently to loath oneself for one's "Abominations". Second, repentance meant a turning *from* sin, the devil, and the darkness of the life of nature, *to* God, goodness, holiness, and grace. Finally, repentance involved a change of the mind itself. There were two stages involved in this repentance; these were likened by Bunyan to the stairs leading to the chambers of Solomon's temple (I Kings vi. 8; and Ezek. xli. 7):

> That by which we turn from nature to grace, and that by which we turn from the imperfections which attend a state of grace, to glory. Hence true repentance, or the right going up these turning Stairs, is called repentance to salvation; for true repentance stopeth [*sic*] not at the reception of grace, for that is but a going up these Stairs to the middle Chambers. . . .[15]

True repentance, in other words, was a continuing, life-long act which brought the sinner from nature to grace, and the saint from grace to perfect glory.

The fruits of repentance were numerous and included a continuing hatred of and shame for sin, the confession of sin, restitution, the amendment of one's life, a contrite spirit, and a fear of and respect for the word and its ministers. A repentance that produced such fruits was regarded as one of the first steps of a genuine profession of faith and one without which there could be no pardon for sin.

The Divine Reply: Justification

AS for this Coat that is on my back, it was given me by the Lord of the place whither I go; and that . . . to cover my nakedness with. And I take it as a token of his kindness to me, for I had nothing but rags before. And besides, thus I comfort my self as I go: Surely, think I, when I come to the Gate of the City, the Lord thereof will know me for good, since I have his Coat on my back; a Coat that he gave me freely in the day that he stript me of my rags.

The granting of this coat—the righteousness of Christ—to Christian was God's act of justifying the sinner. To wear this coat (or to be justified) meant that one had been acquitted by the law before God and in "the Court of Conscience", and had been pronounced just. More specifically, justification before God, on the one hand, "is, when a man stands clear, quit, free, or, in a saved Condition before him, in the Approbation of his holy Law". Justification before men, on the other hand, "is, when a Man stands clear and quit from just ground of Reprehension with them". To be clothed in such a garment was to be freed from the guilt of sin, the condemnation of the law, and the punishment of eternal damnation.[16]

Bunyan was typically Calvinist in regarding justification as acquittal and the pronouncing of the sinner just. Such a concept was also found in the writings of Owen, Thomas Goodwin, and Ussher. According to the Arminian John Goodwin, however, justification involved the forgiveness of sin as much as it did the imputation of righteousness.[17] Many Calvinists broadened the scope of justification to include this element of forgiveness, but without regarding it as fundamentally part of the act of justification *per se*. Bunyan himself considered justification and forgiveness two separate and distinct acts, as did the Baptist Thomas

Collier. At the opposite extreme were the Socinians, who defined justification solely in terms of the forgiveness of sins.[18]

Bunyan followed the classic Protestant doctrine of justification by repeatedly stressing that it was an act of grace alone. God "justifies us, by bestowing upon us, not by expecting from us. He justifies us by his Grace, not by our Works." As was true in so many other cases Bunyan here made Pauline thought the basis for his doctrine of justification *sola gratia*. Because justification was by grace it was a free and sovereign act of God, for "grace can justifie freely, when it will, who it will, from what it will".[19]

Because justification was by grace alone it was solely the act of God and was not in any way dependent on any righteousness or good act of which the sinner was capable; justification was "without the least precedent Qualification of ours." Justification did not in any way involve man's obedience to the law, contrary to the assertion of the Quaker Edward Burrough that such obedience was necessary for justification. "The First Cause . . . of Justification before God", Bunyan later argued,

> dependeth upon the Will of God, who will Justifie, because he will: Therefore, the meritorious Cause [which was the righteousness of Christ] must also be of his own providing, else his Will cannot herein be Absolute: For if Justification depend upon our personal Performances, then not upon the Will of God. . . .

To prove his point Bunyan referred to the parable of the prodigal son (Luke xv. 11–32), noting that the robe bestowed upon him when he returned home (i.e., the righteousness by which he was justified), "being in the Father's House, was not in the Prodigal's Heart. . . ." Man was, in essence, passive in the work of justification, for "to be made righteous, implies a passiveness in him that is so made, and the activity of the work to lie in some body else. . . ."[20]

If justification viewed from the divine perspective was justification *sola gratia*, viewed from the human perspective it was justification *sola fide*. For Bunyan to say this was not to detract in any way from his belief that justification was solely God's act and thus *sola gratia*, for faith itself was wholly dependent on the working of God in the elect. What faith had to do in justification was not to produce works for that justification but "to expect Justification by Grace, through him [i.e., Christ] . . ."

> For we are justified by Faith; not . . . as it is a Grace, nor . . . as it is an acting Grace; but by the righteousness of Faith; that is, by that righteousness that Faith embraceth, layeth hold of, and helpeth the Soul to rest upon, and to trust to, for justification. . . .

Baxter rejected the idea embraced by Bunyan that faith justified as it was the receiving of Christ's righteousness alone. He insisted instead that there be a comparable emphasis on accepting Christ as sanctifier, teacher, ruler, judge, and example, and on consenting to be obedient. The Arminian John Goodwin attributed considerably more importance to the role of faith in justification than did any of the Calvinists. According to him faith itself justified because it had been "sanctified and established for such a purpose . . ." by God, although there was nothing in faith which necessitated that he do so. The Quakers, for their part, altogether rejected the doctrine of justification by faith alone.[21]

According to Bunyan faith was only the instrumental cause (or the sign) and not the meritorious cause of justification. Its role in justifying the sinner was only "Relative" to the justifying righteousness of Christ; apart from that to which it was relative faith merited nothing. It was true, Bunyan admitted, that the believer's "faith is counted for righteousness" (Rom. iv. 5), but only in the sense that "it seals to the Truth of the sufficiency of the Righteousness of Christ, and giveth all the Glory to God. . . ." Such an interpretation was defended at length by Owen and was contrary to the Arminian position. According to John Goodwin, "God requires Faith in the Gospel for the same end for which he required works or perfect righteousnes in the Law. . . ." Consequently, Goodwin explained, for God to impute this faith for that righteousness was for him to accept it as if it were the required legal righteousness.[22]

The Quaker William Penn went one step beyond the Arminian

position of John Goodwin in his opposition to "the dark Imputarians of this age". Penn contended that justification was not from the imputation of another's righteousness, but from the actual keeping by the believer of God's commandments. Bunyan could not agree at all. For him man was in no sense justified or even partially justified by keeping certain precepts or laws. "The Law and the Works thereof, . . . must by us be cast away; not only because they here [in justification] are useless, but also they being retained, are an hindrance." This was one of the points of controversy between Bunyan and Fowler; Fowler had asserted that

> seeing the great end of the Gospel is to make men good, what pretence can there be for thinking, that Faith is the [only] Condition . . . of Justification, as it complieth with only the precept of relying on Christ's Merits for the obtaining of it: especially when it is no less manifest than . . . that obedience to the other precepts must go before obedience to this. . . .

Bunyan's rejection of this argument in favour of one which made justification dependent on faith or reliance on Christ's righteousness alone was attacked by Fowler as an overemphasis on imputed righteousness at the expense of moral righteousness.[23]

Bunyan was also adamant in rejecting the idea that sinners were justified by following the example or pattern set by Christ for that purpose. Such a position had been advocated by Penn when he wrote that "unless we become doers of that Law, which Christ came . . . as our Example, to fulfil, we can never be justified before God. . . ." Fowler's statement that "Christ was an example of all those vertues or graces that qualifie men for the Kingdom of God . . ." might also be interpreted in such a manner. Bunyan made his position clear by affirming that "Justification with God, comes not by imitating Christ as exemplary in Morals, but through Faith in his Precious Blood". Other alternatives to justification *sola fide* were no more acceptable. Men could not be justified by following, as the Quakers purportedly asserted, the Inner Light.[24] Neither could justification (at least in God's sight) be said to involve works in any way, either in combination with faith or as righteous deeds performed after the first act of faith. Yet most Calvinist writers, although agreeing that sinners were justified without good works, nevertheless asserted their necessity for salvation.[25] They were therefore closer to the actual thought of Calvin than was Bunyan, who here followed Luther very closely. Calvin's own position was that men were not justified by works, but neither were they justified without works.

In asserting his concept of justification by faith alone Bunyan regarded faith primarily as the instrumental cause of justification, so that justification was subsequent in sequence to faith. This position was expressed in both of his major treatises on justification (published in 1672 and, posthumously, in 1692) as well as in incidental passages dealing with justification in various of his other writings. It was, of course, possible to say (without being unorthodox) that the elect were justified "in the sight and foreknowledge of God before the foundation of the world. . . ." Faith too could be regarded as something accomplished in the foreknowledge of God before creation, hence there was no real reversal of the traditional sequence. It was also possible to say that because Christ was a common or public person the elect were "justified in his Justification . . ." but this as well was regarded as orthodox doctrine.[26]

By 1685, however, Bunyan had clearly adopted the Antinomian position on the relation of faith to justification when he advocated that "a man may be justified before God, even then when himself knoweth nothing thereof, . . . and so when, and while he hath not Faith about it. . . ." Instead of being a single act justification now had to be regarded as having a distinctly dual aspect: "There is a Justification by Faith, by Faiths applying of that righteousness to the Understanding and Conscience, which God hath afore of his Grace imputed for righteousness to the Soul for Justification in his sight." To assert such a theory did not, in the eyes of Bunyan, mean a rejection of the necessity of faith inasmuch as God willed that those whom he had justified have faith in order that "they may know and believe the things not onely that shall be, but that already Are, freely given to us of God". Bunyan argued for this new concept of justification with all the intensity of conviction with which he had previously argued for the traditional concept: "To say, That an unjustified Man, has Faith . . . is to overthrow the Gospel. For what need of Christs Righteousness, if a Man may have Faith and the Spirit of Christ without it. . . ."[27]

Although he changed his mind on the question of the proper sequence of faith and justification, Bunyan remained unswerving in his conviction that the justification of the sinner was accomplished solely by the imputation of Christ's righteousness. Imputation was defined as the reckoning or accounting of something to someone; thus the imputation of Christ's righteousness meant "Gods making of it ours by an Act of his Grace . . .," but without our becoming "really and personally . . . that which is imputed unto . . ." us. This was the position of strict Calvinists and Antinomians.[28] Baxter, as a moderate Calvinist, would accept the idea that Christ's righteousness was imputed to the believer only if such a phase meant that "the Covenant of Grace doth as certainly . . . justifie us . . . for the merit of Christs Righteousness . . . as our own merit (had it been possible) would have done. . . ." This was very close to the Arminian position, the essence of which was that a believer was justified for the sake of Christ's righteousness without that righteousness being in any way made his own. The essential difference between the Antinomian and strict Calvinist position on the one hand and the moderate Calvinist and Arminian position on the other was that the former accepted an actual imputation of righteousness whereas the latter asserted that a believer's faith was accepted in lieu of righteousness because of the righteousness of Christ. Penn made no attempt to maintain the doctrine by such semantic subterfuge; for him "Justification by an Imputative Righteousness . . . [was] meerly an imagination, not a reality. . . ."[29]

Bunyan rejected Fowler's contention (which was also that of moderate Calvinists and Arminians) that justification meant "dealing with sincerely righteous persons, as if they were perfectly so, for the sake . . . of Christ's Righteousness". For God to have done this, Bunyan argued, would have been for him to justify "their imperfect Righteousness First, and so Secondarily their Persons for the sake of that". It was instead the case that the righteousness with which sinners were justified was God's and not their own, for "if I work for justifying righteousness, and that way get righteousness, my Justification is not of Grace but of Debt. . . ." Fowler was consequently criticised for denying that the righteousness with which the sinner was justified was, in Bunyan's words, "a Righteousness of God's appointing, not of his Prescribing us; a Righteousness that Intirely is Included in the Person of Christ".[30]

Here, then, was the centre of the vituperative controversy between Bunyan and Fowler. The thesis of Fowler's treatise on *The Design of Christianity* was that the purpose of Christ's work was the reformation of men's lives, the purification of their natures, and their restoration to the perfect righteousness which they originally possessed in Adam. "The free Grace of God," he felt, was "infinitely more magnified, in renewing our Natures, than it could be in the bare justification of our persons. . . ." Fowler's pronounced emphasis on sanctification and moral righteousness was countered by Bunyan with an equally pronounced emphasis on justification and imputed righteousness. Christ, Bunyan wrote,

hath not designed to Promote, or to Perfect that righteousness that is Founded on, and Floweth from, the Purity of our Humane Nature: for then he must design the setting up [of] Mans righteousness; that which is of the Law: and then he must design also the setting up of that which is directly in opposition, both also, to the Righteousness, that of God is designed to Justifie us: and that by which we are inwardly made Holy.

Fowler's concern with the restoration of man's original righteousness by Christ was regarded by Bunyan as a threat to what he considered to be the true Christian doctrine of justification by the imputed righteousness of Christ alone.[31]

The nature of this imputed righteousness, which was the meritorious cause of justification, consisted of the obedience of

Christ, not of the removal of the imperfections of man's own righteousness by grace. The righteousness of Christ imputed to the sinner involved both the former's active and passive obedience. This righteousness was "by God accounted the mans that shall accept thereof by faith. . . ." Even when imputed to the elect, however, this righteousness was "yet personally his, not ours", "even as the Wing and Feathers still abide in the Hen, when the Chickens are covered, kept, and warmed thereby". Christ's righteousness could be considered that of the elect only when they were thought of as being in union with him or to the extent that it was "fulfilled in that common Nature which the Son of God took of the Virgin". When Fowler suggested that the holiness which was the design of Christianity was "not such as is Subjected in any thing without us, or is made ours by a meer External application . . .", Bunyan retorted that the holiness and righteousness of saints was that of the Son of God, and that no man possessed any measure of that righteousness except as he was united with the Son through faith.[32]

Not only was the righteousness of Christ that of the believer by virtue of his union with Christ, but that righteousness was also imputed to him while he was ungodly. Fowler had contended that this righteousness could not be imputed to an unrighteous man since "it would signifie as little to his happiness, while he continueth so, as would a gorgeous and splendid garment to one that is almost starved with hunger. . . ." The Quakers agreed. Bunyan, however, argued that it would be superfluous for God to impute the righteousness of Christ to one who was already righteous. Apart from that, Bunyan contended, Paul had clearly stated that God justified the ungodly (Rom. iv. 5). Fowler in turn asserted that the meaning of Rom. iv. 5 was that "God justifies those that were once ungodly, not while they are ungodly: God . . . cannot pass a false judgment, and declare those Righteous, that are utterly void of Righteousness. . . ." At the root of this problem of interpretation was a divergence of opinion on the fundamental question of the purpose of imputation. For Bunyan there could be no release for the ungodly from the curse of sin and the awesome wrath of God apart from the imputation of the perfect righteousness of Christ since that alone would satisfy the holiness and justice of God. Fowler, on the other hand, was convinced that the purpose of the imputation of Christ's righteousness was to "excite men in their endeavours after such a Righteousness as this is"; this would be possible only if men were "sincerely, through his grace, willing and desirous to leave their Sins . . .", and hence not ungodly.[33]

It was not sufficient, according to Bunyan, for men merely to be accounted righteous. God made a man righteous by "putting the Righteousness of God upon him". Thus it could be said with certainty that "if Men be made righteous, they are so. . . ." They were consequently righteous according to the law, because if they had been made righteous "by a Righteousness which the Law commendeth [as it does the perfect righteousness of Christ], how can Fault be found with them by the Law?" Having been made righteous there was then "infused a principle of Grace into the heart . . ." or, in other words, a principle of righteousness which enabled the believer to live a holy life. His justification in the sight of God was complete and perfect, although "it maketh us not perfect with inherent perfection". Although he remained imperfect in the sight of men, the believer could, because of the principle of righteousness which had been infused in him, produce the good works that were necessary to prove his justification to them.[34]

The Divine Reply: Forgiveness

RIVERS yield continually fresh and new Water. . . . And thus it is with the River of God which is full of Water; it yieldeth continually fresh Supplies, fresh and new Supplies of Grace to those that have Business in these Waters. And this is the reason that when Sin is pardoned, it seems as if it were carried away.[35]

In the salvation process forgiveness could only be granted to the sinner after he had been justified, for "a promise of remission of sins supposeth a Righteousness . . . going before; for there is no forgiveness of sins, nor promise of forgiveness, but for the sake of righteousness. . . ." That righteousness could only be the imputed righteousness of Christ. God, according to Bunyan, could not pardon a man devoid of Christ's imputed righteousness because such an act would counter God's promised judgement of damnation for the unrighteous. William Penn, on the other hand, argued that if Christ's righteousness had been imputed to sinners, there would have been nothing left for God to forgive. This was also the Socinian position.[36]

Forgiveness of sins was made possible, according to Bunyan, only because of the atoning satisfaction of Christ which enabled the sinner to be forgiven by law, thereby not wronging divine justice. "Upon the square . . . of the worthiness of the Blood of Christ, Grace Acts, and offers Forgiveness of Sin to Men. . . ." Fowler had written that Christ died only "to put us into a Capacity of pardon . . .", but for Bunyan this was not sufficient. According to him Christ died "to put us into the Personal Possession of Pardon . . .; and that before we know it". Furthermore, in opposition to Fowler's contention that forgiveness was not absolutely procured by Christ's death but by faith and obedience, Bunyan retorted that the death of Christ effectually obtained forgiveness for all the elect even before they were reconciled to their maker. For such forgiveness Bunyan stipulated that faith was necessary, for it was the task of faith to apply that forgiveness to the pilgrim. Faith itself, however, did not merit forgiveness, nor was the believer forgiven for the sake of his repentance. It was all a matter of grace.[37]

According to Bunyan, there could be no forgiveness of sins without a broken heart and a contrite spirit, yet sin was "forgiven us freely by Grace, and not for the sake of our amendments. . . ." It was derogatory to free grace to assert, as Fowler did, that only "holy Souls . . . are capable of having the Guilt of their Sins removed . . .", and that it was impossible for a wicked man to have his sins forgiven. God, Bunyan argued in reply, pardoned the sins of the wicked "not because they have made themselves Holy, or have given up themselves to the Law of Nature, or to the

Dictates of their Humane Principles, but because he will be Gracious, and because he will give to . . . Christ the benefit of his Blood". The glory of grace was that "God doth not use to Pardon Painted Sinners, but such as are Really so". Forgiveness brought the pilgrim psychological peace through the removing of the guilt complex previously implanted by a zealous preacher. Bunyan used a medical analogy to make his point more vivid: "For as a Leaf for Medicine, when applied to a sore in the body doth supple, molify, and heal the wound; so the word of Promise when rightly applyed to the soul, it doth supple, molify and heal the wounded conscience". The result was, for Bunyan, clearly a sense of inner peace and "the beginning of Health to the Soul. . . ."[38]

The Divine Reply: Sanctification

THEN he [i.e., Emmanuel] commanded that the Image of Diabolus should be taken down from the place where it was set up; and that they should destroy it utterly. . . . And that the Image of Shaddai his Father should be set up again, with his own, upon the Castle gates. . . .

After this was done, Em[m]anuel gave out a Commandment that those three great Diabolonians should be apprehended, namely the two late Lord Mayors, to wit, Mr. Incredulity, Mr. Lustings, and Mr. Forget good the Recorder. Besides these, there were some of them that Diabolus made Burgesses and Aldermen in Mansoul. . . .

And these were their names, Alderman Atheism, Alderman Hardheart, and Alderman False-peace. The Burgesses were Mr. Notruth, Mr. Pitiless, Mr. Haughty, with the like. These were committed to close custody. . . .

After this the Prince gave a charge that the three strong holds that at the command of Diabolus the Diabolonians built in Mansoul, should be demolished. . . .

So the Town of Mansoul slew them according to the word of their Prince. . . .[39]

The process of the cleansing of the town of Mansoul was, in

theological terminology, the sanctification of the justified sinner.

The promise of sanctification, Bunyan informed his readers, went hand in hand with effectual calling. He would have agreed with Owen's description of election as the spring of sanctification. As part of the process of salvation, sanctification was, for Bunyan, the consequence of justification and was subsequent too to forgiveness. Apart from sanctification there could be no salvation; "whoever pretends to Justification, if he be not Sanctified, pretends to what he is not. . . ." Sanctification was made possible by the atoning work of Christ solely because of grace. Believers were, according to Bunyan, sanctified through the operation of the Spirit.

> The Holy Ghost is sent into our Hearts, not to Excite us to a Compliance with our Old and Wind-shaken Excellencies, that came into the World with us, but to Write new Laws in our Hearts; even the Law of Faith, the Word of Faith, and of Grace, and the Doctrine of Remission of Sins, . . . that Holiness might flow from thence.

From man's standpoint all of this could be accomplished only by faith. Without such faith not even good works would sanctify.[40]

Sanctification in God's sight was complete because the believer was sanctified in Christ.

> First we are sanctified in his flesh, as we are justified by his righteousness. Wherefore he [i.e., Christ] is that holy one that setteth us, in himself, a holy lump before God, not only with reference to Justification and Life, but with reference to Sanctification and Holiness. . . .

In themselves, however, believers were not perfectly holy even though they were sanctified. The possibility and the actuality of sin remained throughout their lives, although it was also true that sanctification changed the whole man—understanding, will, mind, affections, judgement, and conscience. "Grace leaves no power, faculty, or passion of the soul unsanctified; wherefore there is no corner in a sanctified soul, where sin may hide his head. . . ." This was not to say that the believer was made entirely perfect or sinless by sanctifying grace, but rather that sin could not exist in the sanctified man "without controul". As Owen expressed the same idea, "Grace and Sin may be in the same Soul at the same time; but they cannot bear Rule in the same Soul at the same time". It was therefore necessary, observed Bunyan, that the justified sinner be continually supplied with sanctifying grace if he was to lead a life of holiness acceptable to God.[41]

The actual sanctifying of the believer by the Spirit was accomplished by "possessing him with a principle of Righteousness: which principle is not of Nature, but of Grace. . . ." This principle of righteousness enabled the pilgrim to accomplish righteous acts which would otherwise be impossible; it was the source of all his good works. The Spirit "principles us in all the Powers of our Souls, with that which is Righteousness in the habit and nature of it". In addition, by the Spirit the believer was "qualified with Principles, not Natural, but Spiritual . . .", and these principles or graces—especially faith, hope, and love—worked to purify him from wickedness. The result of this sanctification was a holy life. and holiness in turn was the pilgrim's path to life eternal.[42]

Persevering to the End

INTERPRETER took Christian . . . into a place, where was a Fire burning against a Wall, and one standing by it always, casting much Water upon it to quench it: Yet did the Fire burn higher and hotter.

. . . This fire is the Work of Grace that is wrought in the heart; he that casts Water upon it, to extinguish and put it out, is the Devil: but in that thou seest the fire notwithstanding burn higher and hotter, thou shalt also see the reason of that: So he had him about to the back side of the Wall, where he saw a Man with a Vessel of Oyl in his hand, of the which he did also continually cast, but secretly, into the fire.[43]

The man standing behind the wall, almost out of sight of tempted souls, was Christ, and the oil which he poured on the fire was the grace which continually maintained the work of salvation in the believer. This illustration depicted God's act of preserving the elect, who persevered through grace. In allegorical language this was Bunyan's answer to one of the principal questions of religious controversy which divided the Calvinists and the Arminians: was it possible for a true believer to fall completely from grace and thereby lose his salvation?

Arminians and Calvinists agreed that true believers who remained such throughout their lives could not fall out of God's favour. Where they differed was over the Arminian contention that a true believer at one stage in life might later cease to believe, and so would fall from divine favour. The Quakers rejected the Calvinist doctrine of perseverance, but with the qualification that (in the words of Robert Barclay) "such an increase and stability in the Truth may, in this life, be attained, from which there can not be a total apostasy". Moderate and strict Calvinists essentially agreed on the doctrine of perseverance, although Baxter emphasised its unimportance, particularly as an object of contention between Arminians and Calvinists. He also stressed man's responsibility to persevere as a condition of salvation more than did the strict Calvinists.[44]

For Bunyan preservation (the divine perspective) and perseverance (the human perspective) were as necessary to salvation as was justification. Preservation was defined by Bunyan as "a saving of us by preserving us, by delivering of us from all those hazards that we run betwixt our state of Justification, and our state of Glorification". The basis of preservation and perseverance was grace, for it was by grace that pilgrims were said to be "upheld, supported, and inabled to go through our needy times, as Christians, without which there is no Salvation neither". For the elect grace provided "a sufficiency of all Spiritual Blessings to be Communicated to them at their need, for their preservation in the Faith, and faithful perseverance through this life. . . ." There was a sufficiency of such grace for none but the elect, for the believer's perseverance and preservation were dependent upon his prior election. Thus, with reference to II Chron. iii. 5, Bunyan observed that "in that the Palm-trees were Set on this Wall [of the temple], it may be to shew, that the Elect are fixed in Jesus, and so shall abide for ever".[45]

Preservation and perseverance were not possible apart from the intercessory work of Christ. This in turn was dependent on the conditions undertaken by the Son in the covenant between him and the Father. "The Covenant by which Christ acteth as a Priest, so far as we are concern'd therein, he also himself acteth our part . . .: Wherefore God doth not count that the Covenant is broken, though we sin. . . ." God said, in effect: "Their sins shall not shake my Covenant, with my beloved, nor cause that I for ever should reject them." It was precisely because of Christ's continuous intercession that Bunyan was certain that the covenant could not be broken: "The durableness of his Intercession proves, That the Covenant, in which those that come to God by him, are concerned and wrapt up, is not shaken, broken or made invalid by all their weaknesses and infirmities." The perseverance of the believer, then, was assured because the covenant of grace of which he was a part was "everlasting, not upon the supposition of my obedience, but upon the unchangeable purpose of God, and the efficacy of the obedience of Christ. . . ." After all, the door of the ark was, Bunyan pointed out, shut by God, not Noah (Gen. vii. 16), and "if God shuts in or out, who can alter it?"[46]

Because of the covenant of grace the elect were given the power to enable them to persevere through faith; consequently there was no impediment which could hinder their salvation. The granting of this power to man did not mean that perseverance was his work, however, for ultimately it was dependent on God; perseverance was "managed" by his power. Furthermore, Christ not only had to continue to intercede for the preservation of the believer, but he also had to "mannage that part that is lacking to our Salvation, well, until he has compleated it".[47] The Spirit, too, was involved, for it was his task to preserve and seal the elect until the time of their final redemption (Eph. i. 13–14). The primacy of God in salvation was thus ceaselessly maintained by Bunyan. Yet man was not passive in his perseverance, but by the aid of grace had to continue to believe and accomplish good works.

Those who were once "effectually in Christ", Bunyan asserted, could never lose him—nor could they be lost by him. "Should he lose a member [of his body], he would be disfigured, maimed, dismemb[e]red, imperfect, next to Monstrous." On God's part, he "cannot, will not dissolve the relation which the spirit of adoption hath made 'twixt the Father and the sons. . . ." Those who doubted this truth were warned by Bunyan that their leader was none other than Captain Brimstone. On the other hand, those who were convinced of the truth of preservation and perseverance were warned not to "take courage to live loose lives, under a supposition, that once in Christ, and ever in Christ, and the covenant cannot be broken, nor the relation of Father and Child dissolved. . . ." Those who acted in such a manner were never really part of the covenant of grace. Although Bunyan and all other Calvinist preachers deplored any tendency to loose living arising from the absolute assurance of salvation, the Arminians nevertheless asserted that the Calvinist doctrine of perseverance "layes the reins of security upon the neck of the flesh, and of the old man, in Beleevers; and deprives them of the sharpest bit, which God hath given them wherewith to restrain and curb the unruly and unregenerate part of the Soul, (we mean, the fear and dread of eternal fire.)"[48]

Although it was impossible for the elect to fall completely from grace and lose their salvation, there was a possibility, Bunyan cautioned, of a momentary fall occasioned by sin. A distinction was to be made, according to Bunyan in a reference to the two walls of Jerusalem (Jer. xxxix. 4 and lii. 7), between the wall of "eternal preservation and security from the wrath of God, through the benefits of Christ . . ." and the wall of "special protection and safeguard that the Church hath always had from and by the special Providence of her God. . . ." The latter wall could be broken down as the result of sin, but the wall of eternal preservation and security always remained steadfast. Like the Israelite who because of poverty had sold his land and eventually had it restored to him in the year of jubilee (Lev. xxv. 23–28), the believer "who by Sin and Decays in Grace, has forfeited his Place and Inheritance in Heaven . . .," has that inheritance returned to him in the world to come. For the most part the believer was prevented from falling by divine power, although when he did fall "into the ditch" between the two walls it was grace which restored him to God's favour through forgiveness. "So many times as the soul backslides, so many times God brings him again, (I mean, the soul that must be saved by grace,) he renews his Pardons. . . ."[49]

Implicit in the last sentence was a warning by Bunyan that not all those who fall are of the elect and will be restored by grace. Elsewhere Bunyan made this explicit: "It is he that holdeth out to the end that must be saved, it is he that overcometh that shall inherit all things, 'tis not every one that begins." Consequently a warning had to be given

> to them that think they stand upon their feet. Give not way to falling because everlasting arms are underneath. . .: God can let thee fall into mischief . . . and not help thee up. . . . I doubt there are many that have presumed upon this mercy, that thus do couch beneath, and have cast themselves down from their pin[n]acles into vanity, of a vain conceit that they shall be lifted up again: whom yet God will leave to dye there, because their fall was rather of wilfulness, than weakness, and of stub[b]ornness, and desperate resolutions, than for want of means and helps to preserve them from it.

Their falling was also attributed to not having had or not retaining the true knowledge of Christ and to not believing in the atoning work which he accomplished. Few who fell in such a manner would ever return to God again. The name by which such a person was ordinarily known, said Bunyan, was Turn-away, but with Turn-away on the pilgrimage were others prone to the same act of falling—Simple, Sloth, Presumption, Formalist, Hypocrisy, Timorous, Mistrust, Discontent, Talkative, By-ends, Hold-the-world, Money-love, and Save-all. Those who did fall away were never true believers and God could not be criticised for not preventing their fall, for "he is a free agent to do what he pleaseth, and may . . . suffer some to fall away, and keep others. . . ."[50]

Although a believer could not persevere apart from divine grace, and even though his preservation was assured because of his election, he was nevertheless urged by Bunyan to press forward strenuously as if he himself were ultimately responsible for the successful completion of his pilgrimage.

> There belonged to this Court [of Solomon's temple] several Gates, an East, a South, and a North Gate; and when the People of the Land went into this Court to worship, they were not to go out at that Gate by which they came in, but out of the Gate over against it, to shew that true Christians should persevere right on, and not turn back, what ever they meet with in the way.

"It is an easy matter for a Man to Run hard for a spurt, for a Furlong, for a Mile or two: O but to hold out for a Hundred, for a Thousand, for Ten Thousand Miles. . . ." It was, indeed, a long, long pilgrimage, and it ended only with the glorious resurrection of the pilgrim as the last step on his soteriological journey.[51]

NOTES

1. XXII, p. 337.
2. LVI, p. 574; VI, p. 16; XXIII, p. 42; XXXII, sect. 143; XII, p. 215; XXXVIII, p. 78; XI, p. 137; XII, p. 117.
3. J. Goodwin, *Remedie*, pp. 7–8; *Redemption Redeemed*, pp. 433, 499–500; *Agreement*, pp. 35–37; Baxter, *Catholick Theologie*, Bk. I, pt. 2, chap. ciii; Collier, *Body of Divinity*, p. 120.
4. XII, p. 218; LVII, Vol. II, p. 52.
5. VI, p. 15; XLIII, p. 391 (cf. Luther, *Galathians*, fol. 243 *verso*); VI, pp. 18–19; XVI, sect. 99 (cf. Talon, *John Bunyan*, p. 77); Luther, *Galathians*, fol. 65 *verso*.
6. Luther, *Galathians*, fol. 177 *verso*; Baxter, *Catholick Theologie*, Bk. I, pt. 2, chap. lxvii; T. Goodwin, *Works*, I, pt. 1, p. 390; *Westminster Confession* (1648 ed.), XIV, ii; Saltmarsh, *Free-Grace*, pp. 94, 156, 192; Dent, *Path-Way*, p. 401; Bayly, *Pietie*, pp. 735–36; Owen, *Person of Christ*, p. 71.
7. XLIII, p. 392; XII, p. 219; Baxter, *Catholick Theologie*, Bk. I, pt. 2, chaps. lxvii and cx; Barclay, *Apology*, p. 16; XXIII, p. 44; Collier, *Body of Divinity*, p. 141; XLIII, p. 391.
8. XXXIX, pp. 39, 213–14.

9. VIII, p. 62; XXXVII, p. 191; XVIII, p. 208 (cf. Luther, *Galathians,* fol. 177 *verso*).
10. Luther, *Galathians,* fol. 116; VI, p. 13; VII, p. 269; XII, pp. 117–18; XIV, pp. 249–50; XXVIII, p. 77.
11. XII, p. 379 (cf. T. Goodwin, *Works,* IV, pt. 3, p. 55ff.); XII, pp. 301, 380; LVI, p. 574.
12. X, p. 12.
13. IV, pp. 22–23.
14. XV, p. 67; XI, p. 156; XII, pp. 64–65, 76–77.
15. XXXVI, p. 86.
16. XXVIII, pp. 40–41 (cf. p. 36); XXVI, p. [99]; LVII, Vol. II, 50; XLVIII, p. 77.
17. Owen, *The Doctrine of Justification by Faith* (1677), p. 171; T. Goodwin, *Works,* I, pt. 2, pp. 279, 297; Ussher, *Body of Divinitie,* p. 194; J. Goodwin, *Impvtatio Fidei,* pt. 1, p. 3, and pt. 2, pp. 5–7, 121–22.
18. T. Goodwin, *Works,* I, pt. 1, p. 91; Owen, *Salus Electorum,* p. 141; Gouge, *Principles,* pp. 13–14; XI, pp. 113, 118, 128; and, for the Socinian position, see the refutation of their concept by Owen, *Justification by Faith,* p. 171.
19. XLIII, p. 385; LII, p. 186; XLI, pp. 52–53.
20. XLVIII, p. 87; Burrough, *Truth (the Strongest of All)* (1657), p. 55 (cf. Penn, *Sandy Foundation,* p. 29); XLVIII, pp. 85, 88; XI. p. 108.
21. XLVIII, p. 98; XI, p. 106; Baxter, *Catholick Theologie,* Bk. I, pt. 2, chaps. cxvii–cxviii; J. Goodwin, *Romans,* pp. 164, 133; Penn, *Sandy Foundation,* p. 28; Barclay, *Apology,* pp. 140, 144–45.
22. XLVIII, p. 84; LIV, p. 261; XLVIII, p. 84; Owen, *Justification by Faith,* pp. 458–62; J. Goodwin, *Impvtatio Fidei,* pt. 1, pp. 15–16.
23. Penn, *Sandy Foundation,* pp. 30, 25; XLVIII, p. 78; Fowler, *Design,* pp. 222–23; VIII, pp. 78–79, 104; Fowler, *Dirt,* p. 68.
24. Penn, *Sandy Foundation,* p. 26; Fowler, *Dirt,* pp. 49–50; VIII, p. 108; cf. Fox, *Journal* (1911 ed.), I, 144.
25. Cf. Bayly, *Pietie,* pp. 233, 983; Owen, *The Chamber of Imagery* (1712; written, 1682), p. 47; Collier, *Body of Divinity,* pp. 184–85.
26. XL, p. 41; LIII, p. 417.
27. XI, pp. 135–36; XLIV, p. 234.
28. XI, p. 131; XLVIII, pp. 78, 85; cf. Bayly, *Pietie,* pp. 132–33, 693, 987–88; Owen, *Justification by Faith,* Chaps. X and XVI; T. Goodwin, *Works,* IV, pt. 1, p. 104; Saltmarsh, *Free-Grace,* p. 176; John Eaton, *The Honey-Combe of Free Justification* (1642), pp. 7, 20.
29. Baxter, *Catholick Theologie,* Bk. I, pt. 2, chap. cxix; J. Goodwin,

Impvtatio Fidei, pt. 1, pp. 7–9, 12, 17; Penn, *Sandy Foundation,* pp. 32–33.
30. Fowler, *Design,* pp. 225–26; VIII, p. 81; XI, p. 124; VIII, p. 75 (referring to Fowler, *Design,* pp. 221–22).
31. Fowler, *Design,* p. 130; VIII, p. 35 (cf. p. 7).
32. VIII, p. 17; XLVIII, p. 78 (cf. Luther, *Galathians,* fol. 112); XLVIII, p. 79; Fowler, *Design,* p. 5; VIII, p. 27.
33. Fowler, *Design,* p. 120; Penn, *Sandy Foundation,* pp. 24–25; Barclay, *Apology,* p. 151; VIII, pp. 60–61; Fowler, *Dirt,* p. 45; VIII, p. 61; Fowler, *Design,* p. 226, and *Dirt,* p. 44.
34. XLIV, p. 233; XLII, p. 131; VI, p. 121; XLIII, p. 377.
35. XLI, pp. 22–23.
36. XI, pp. 128, 118; Penn, *Sandy Foundation,* p. 30; and, for a refutation of the Socinian position, see Owen, *Justification by Faith,* pp. 297–98.
37. XV, p. 91; Fowler, *Design,* p. 91; VIII, pp. 33, 31–32, 39–40.
38. XI, p. 159; Fowler, *Design,* pp. 31, 119; VIII, p. 60; XLVI, p. 211; XX, pp. 280–81; XII, p. 258.
39. XXII, pp. 183–84, 210.
40. Owen, *Person of Christ,* p. 51; XLIV, p. 236; XXXVIII, pp. 23, 25; VIII, p. 68.
41. LIII, p. 418; XXI, p. 108; Owen, *Sin and Grace,* p. 21.
42. XLIV, p. 234; VIII, p. 8.
43. XXVIII, pp. 25–26.
44. J. Goodwin, *et al., Agreement,* pp. 66–67; Barclay, *Apology,* p. 184; Baxter, *Catholick Theologie,* Bk. I, pt. 2, pp. 9, 12, 19, and chap. cccxxxix, and Bk. II, pp. 198, 208.
45. XLIII, p. 373; LIV, p. 287; LVI, p. 560; XXXVI, p. 77.
46. XLIII, p. 394; XXXIX, p. 60 (cf. Bayly, *Pietie,* p. 902); XLV, p. 50 (referring also to Rev. iii. 7).
47. XLIII, p. 381.
48. XVI, sect. 107; XLII, p. 102; LIV, p. 283; XXXIX, p. 74; XXII, p. 294; XXXIX, p. 73; J. Goodwin, *et. al., Agreement,* p. 72 (cf. p. 76).
49. XX, p. 61; XLII, p. 143; XX, p. 62; LVI, p. 568.
50. XIX, p. 57; LIII, p. 407; XXI, pp. 55–56; XII, p. 216.
51. XXXVI, pp. 21–22 (referring to Ezek. xlvi. 9); XIX, p. 33.

4 The Pilgrim's Covenant

THOSE WHO ACCEPTED the concept of predestination were immediately confronted with the realisation that their eternal destination had long ago been determined. In the face of such a realisation there might logically have resulted a pronounced feeling of passivity and resignation to the inevitable fate. Yet those who firmly adhered to the Calvinist tradition could not psychologically embrace such passivity and resignation. Pascal's willingness to confront throughout life a perpetual state of doubt, concern, and hence misery was not shared by Calvinists. Instead they sought in themselves manifestations of divine election which might serve to comfort them with regard to any uncertainty about the future life. Simultaneously they could look for the lack of those signs in others, as Bunyan did in Mr. Badman, the representative reprobate. Seeing the absence of signs pointing to election in those Englishmen whose wealth and social status were a source of resentment to the sectaries must have provided some psychological comfort. Nevertheless, sectaries and Puritans alike were concerned more with their own election than with their adversaries' reprobation. In order to understand better the dealings of the Calvinistic God with man, English Puritans and sectaries developed an elaborate covenant theology. That theology specified precisely what conditions were required on both sides in order for man to be accepted by God. Precisely what those conditions were and how they were to be fulfilled provoked considerable dispute in the century of revolution.

The elucidation of the covenant scheme, centring around the personal relationship of the divine to the human, was a task assumed almost wholly by the exponents of Calvinist theology. The Arminians, while adopting the covenant idea itself, nevertheless adapted it to harmonise with the rest of their theology, so that the covenant of grace became no more than simply the offer of grace to anyone willing to accept it. In biblical terms, as John Goodwin indicated, this was expressed by Mark xvi. 16 or John vi. 37. Even less interest in the covenant idea was shown by the Quakers, whose mystic tendencies led them to formulate their understanding of the relationship between the divine and human in terms of the Inner Light.

Bunyan himself expounded covenant thought for the first time in 1659 as *The Doctrine of the Law and Grace Unfolded*. To understand his place in the covenant tradition, it is necessary to understand first of all something of the basic rudiments which make up that tradition. Generally speaking, covenant theologians can be classified into three groups. At one end of the continuum were the moderate Calvinists, whose ideas were more akin to the Zwingli-Bullinger-Tyndale tradition than to those of Calvin, William Perkins and William Ames, particularly with regard to the necessity of the fulfilment of the covenant conditions on man's part and the ensuing ethical responsibility (particularly as set forth in the moral law) which participation in the covenant meant.

The remaining two groups were closer to the Calvinist tradition in their emphasis on God's role in establishing the covenant, particularly in enduing the elect with the necessary grace, or even accomplishing all the conditions for them, perhaps as they were represented by the Son when the covenant of grace was first formulated between him and the Father before creation. The primary feature which distinguished these two groups was their attitude toward the moral law. On the one hand there were the strict Calvinists, who argued that the moral law had a rightful and necessary place in the life of the Christian, and on the other hand there were the Antinomians who tended to advocate the abrogation of the law for those who were "under grace". As will be shown, Bunyan himself may be classified with the strict Calvinists, though at times—as in his emphasis on the covenant of grace between the Father and the Son, and in the covenant of grace as being without conditions on man's part—he veered sharply toward the Antinomians.

Although the precise and systematic delineation of this covenant scheme was a subject of considerable disagreement on the part of its seventeenth century proponents, there was at least substantial unity on the matter of defining the nature of a covenant. The covenant by definition was an agreement between two parties based on the fulfilment of certain conditions. In *The Doctrine of the Law and Grace Unfolded* Bunyan defined the covenant as having three parts:

> First, what it is, that is covenanted for.
> Secondly, the conditions, upon which the persons, who are concerned in it, do agree.
> Thirdly, if the conditions on both sides be not according to the agreement fulfilled: then the Covenant standeth not, but is made void.[1]

This, of course, was fundamentally the classic concept of the covenant (*foedus* or *pactum*) in legal terms, but when it came to defining the precise nature of the biblical terms *berith* and *diatheke*, there was no parallel consensus of opinion (as will subsequently be shown).

The Covenant of Works

> CHRISTIAN turned out of his way to go to Mr. Legality's house for help: but behold, when he was got now hard by the Hill [Mt. Sinai, typifying the law and covenant of works], it seemed so high, and also that side of it that was next the way side, did hang so much over, that Christian was afraid to venture further, lest the Hill should fall on his head. . . . Also his burden, now, seemed heavier to him, than while he was in his way. There came also flashes of fire out of the Hill, that made Christian afraid that he should be burned. . . .[2]

The covenant of works, according to virtually all covenant theologians, was established with Adam in the Garden of Eden while he was yet in a state of innocency, the words of institution being Gen. ii. 16–17. "The Tree of the Knowledge of Good and Evil", Bunyan wrote in his exposition of Gen. i–xi, "was a Type of the Law, or Covenant of Works"—"though possibly not so openly", he elsewhere remarked—"as the sequel of the Story clearly manifesteth; for had not Adam eaten thereof, he had enjoyed for ever his first Blessedness." The conditions involved in this covenant were, on man's part, perfect obedience to the law and abstention from all evil. Conditions were necessary, "for a Covenant of Works cannot be established; that is, settled between God and Men, before both parties have either by Sureties, or performance ratified . . . the same". Man was made capable of fulfilling such exacting conditions, and was promised life if he should do so, but was threatened with death if he failed. It was clearly man's responsiblity to obey God. But by his disobedience, Adam, and all of mankind as they were represented in Adam, broke the covenant and consequently "stood not onely guilty of Sin, by Imputation, but Polluted by the Filth that Possessed him at his fall. . . ." Thus far covenant writers would fundamentally agree.[3]

Once man broke the covenant of works, Bunyan saw fit to describe his newly-fallen nature in terms conforming to the most extreme statements in the Lutheran and Reformed (ultimately, in the Pauline and Augustinian) traditions. Because of original and actual sin—sin being "the breach of the Law"—all men were regarded as totally depraved and devoid of all grace. Adam, by sinning and breaking the covenant, had become "the conduit-pipe through which the Devil did convey of[f] his poisoned spawn and venome nature into the hearts of Adams sons and daughters. . . ."[4]

Man in the covenant scheme, according to Bunyan, whether before or after his act of disobedience, was unavoidably concerned with the divine law. The law as it was originally given to Adam, Bunyan asserted, was in substance the same as was later given to Moses on Mount Sinai, and was in essence natural law.

While it was possible to distinguish between natural and Mosaic law, as did Anthony Burgess in his *Vindiciae Legis: or, A Vindication of the Morall Law and the Covenants* (2nd ed., 1647), Bunyan was concerned only with distinguishing between the two proclamations of the Mosaic law on Mount Sinai.

In making a distinction between the two manifestations of the law Bunyan involved himself in a debate on whether the Mosaic law was part of the covenant of works or the covenant of grace. In a broadside entitled *Of the Law and a Christian* which remained unpublished during his lifetime, he remarked concerning the dual giving of the law: "I think the first doth more principally intend its force as a Covenant of works . . .; but this second time not (at least in the manner of its being given) respecting such a Covenant, but rather as a rule, or directory to those who already are found in the clift of the rock, Christ [Ex. xxxiii. 22]. . . ."[5] Principally, then, the Mosaic law was a restatement of the covenant of works, as Bunyan argued in his 1659 treatise, although he was careful not to exclude its use under the covenant of grace as a rule of life. This, however, is to anticipate, for the issue here was not whether or not the Mosaic law was a rule of life under the covenant of grace, but rather whether or not that law was in fact part of the covenant of grace itself as it was given to Moses. Those who affirmed that it was were the moderate Calvinists,[6] whereas those who, with Bunyan, associated the Mosaic law with the covenant of works were the strict Calvinists, the Antinomians, and even the Arminian John Goodwin.[7]

Writing around 1665, in his treatise on *The Resurrection of the Dead*, Bunyan described the Mosaic law as "the chief, and most pure Resemblance of the Justice and holiness of the Heavenly Majesty, and doth hold forth to all men, the sharpness and keenness of his wrath. . . ." Such language on Bunyan's part was reminiscent not only of Luther's reference to the law as "revealing unto them [i.e., sinners] their sinne, the wrath and judgement of God . . .", but also of the prominent law-grace dichotomy in the whole of Luther's commentary on Galatians. "The Book of the Law wide open, from whence issued a flame of fire," was, for Bunyan, the escutcheon of Captain Conviction in *The Holy War*, and in the *The Pilgrim's Progress* the law was that which made Christian's burden heavier.[8]

Could the law then lead the sinner to Christ? An affirmative answer would imply that it was, at least in some sense, a means of grace. Paul seemingly suggested that it could when he labelled it a "tutor" in Galatians iii. 24, but Bunyan, in his reply to the Quaker Edward Burrough, interpreted this verse as referring only to the ceremonial law—and that in the past tense—and not to the moral law (or Ten Commandments). He indignantly informed Burrough that

> the Moral Law . . . is so far from leading us to Christ by our following it, that it doth even lead those that are led by it under the curse. Not because the Law hath an evil end in it, but because of our weaknesse and inability to do it; therefore it is forced, as it is just, to passe a sentence of condemnation on every one, that in every particular fulfills it not.

In drawing this distinction, however, Bunyan departed from the traditional manner of interpreting Gal. iii. 24 as proof that the moral law did lead men to Christ. Here he did not follow Luther's argument that the law "leaveth not in death and damnation those that are of a contrite heart . . . but driveth them unto Christ".[9]

In any case there was agreement among theologians on the point that no man could achieve salvation by fulfilling the law himself. In an attempt to impress this verity upon children, Bunyan drew their attention to a Moses that was "fair and comely", but yet was unable to make white the blackness of his wife's skin, concluding that

> . . . Moses was a type of Moses Law,
> His Wife likewise one that never saw
> Another way unto eternal Life;
> There's Myst'ry then in Moses and his Wife.
>   The Law is very Holy, Just and good,
> And to it is espous'd all Flesh and Blood:
> But this its Goodness it cannot bestow,
> On any that are wedded thereunto.[10]

The Covenant of Grace: The Divine Aspect

ONLY the King, and his Son foresaw all this [i.e., the capture of Mansoul by Diabolus] long before, yea, and sufficiently provided for the relief of Mansoul . . . . This Son of Shaddai, I say, having stricken hands with his Father, and promised that he would be his servant to recover his Mansoul again, stood by his resolution . . . . The purport of which agreement was this; To wit, That at a certain time prefixed by both, the Kings Son should take a journey into the Countrey of Universe, and there in a way of Justice and equity, by making of amends for the follies of Mansoul, he should lay a foundation of her perfect deliverance from Diabolus . . . .[11]

The covenant of grace was in substance the gracious promise of the free forgiveness of sins—in biblical terms, Hebrews viii. 12. And yet it was more than this, for it "not only concludeth the Matter concerned between the Persons themselves; but it provideth Remedy against after Temptations, and Fears, and Mistrusts, as to the faithful Performance of that which is spoken of . . . ". In this sense, *The Pilgrim's Progress* was Bunyan's detailed testimony to this aspect of the covenant of grace. In this context one can also accept Leonard Trinterud's observation that "Bunyan had woven into the allegorical pilgrimage pattern, so long traditional in English preaching, the whole of the covenant theology's conception of the various stages by which man was regenerated (the *ordo salutis*)".[12]

The covenant of grace in Bunyan's thought, however, was ultimately based not upon this reference which the covenant had to man, but rather upon his belief that the covenant was established in eternity. Of this he was already certain in 1659, when he informed his readers that the covenant of grace "was made between the Father and the Son, long before it was accomplished, or manifestly sealed with Christ's blood, it was made before the world began . . . ". Here, then, is where a discussion of Bunyan's concept of the covenant of grace must begin—precisely with the idea that "the Covenant it self was Christ, as given of God unto us, with all his good Conditions, Merit and Worth".[13]

To call Christ himself the covenant was not an idea peculiar to

Bunyan, for other writers, such as John Saltmarsh, Tobias Crisp, and the author of *The Marrow of Modern Divinity* did likewise, simply using the phraseology of Isaiah xlii. 6 or xlix. 8.[14] That this covenant was the covenant of grace, however, was a matter of considerable dispute. Those who either explicitly or implicitly associated it with the covenant of grace were the Antinomians and the strict Calvinists,[15] whereas the Arminians and the moderate Calvinists made a definite distinction between the two covenants. The Arminian John Goodwin not only denied the identity of the two covenants, but also questioned the very existence of a covenant between the Father and the Son.[16] Baxter, the master conciliator, made a distinction between the covenant of mediation between the Father and the Son, and the covenant of grace between God and man. Presumably to avoid misunderstanding, he preferred to refer to the mediatorial covenant as God's eternal decree of redemption, involving a promise to man. Along the same lines, Rutherford and Blake both denied the identity of the two covenants, but Blake was apparently not appreciative of Baxter's conciliatory theology, and criticised him for apparently asserting the identity of the two covenants. Bunyan knew, in 1659, exactly where he stood on this issue: there could be no doubt that this covenant between Father and Son was the covenant of grace; "this Covenant was not made with God and the creature; . . . this Covenant was made with the second person, with the eternal Word of God. . . ."[17]

The Covenant of Grace: The Human Aspect

WHEN, in *The Pilgrim's Progress*, Christian had journeyed from the City of Destruction to the wicket gate, he inquired of the gatekeeper whether or not he could gain admittance to the way to Mount Zion. The reply he received was from Good Will (one of Bunyan's synonyms for grace): "I am willing with all my heart, said he; and with that he opened the Gate."[18] The point which Bunyan made was clear: it was God—not man—who opened the gate, thus admitting the sinner into the covenant of grace. Did this mean that, for Bunyan, God alone made the covenant, or was the covenant made between God *and* man?

The answer to this question is related to a problem previously posed but left unanswered, for the solution is dependent on the way in which Bunyan conceived of the covenant of grace as it related to man. Was it essentially a pact or a testament, a contract or a promise? This was a key question in covenant thought— perhaps *the* key question, for in ascertaining the various answers given to that question by representative writers, one has a convenient and accurate means of distinguishing between the two principal traditions of Calvinism in the central years of the seventeenth century.

The moderate Calvinists conceived of the covenant more as a pact or contract. Baxter, for example, wrote in 1651 that "the very definition of a proper Covenant . . . sheweth as much that it must be a mutual engagement".[19] For the strict Calvinists and the Antinomians, on the other hand, the covenant assumed more the character of a testament or promise. Archbishop Ussher, whom Baxter admired greatly, provided a good example of this view when he wrote that the covenant of grace was made by "God alone: for properly man hath no more power to make a spirituall Covenant in his naturall estate, then before his creation he had to promise obedience". While Ussher somewhat inconsistently spoke of this covenant as a contract, he nevertheless clearly indicated its promissory rather than contractual nature when he affirmed that "it containeth the free promises of God made unto us in Jesus Christ. . . ." In much the same way Owen stressed the idea that the covenant of grace was made "in the way of a singular and absolute Promise . . .", though he did admit that "we shall enter into a Covenant state with him . . . by the way of the Condition required on our part".[20]

Bunyan, commenting on the covenant of grace as it was manifested to Noah (Gen. ix. 15), opposed the conception of it as a contract, insisting instead on its gratuitous nature:

> We read not here of any Compact or Agreement between Noah and God Almighty; wherefore such Conditions and Compacts could not be the Terms between him and us: What then? why that Covenant that he calls his, which is his gift to us, I will give thee for a Covenant; this is the Covenant which is between God and us: There is one God, and one Mediator between God and Man, the Man Christ Jesus.[21]

Again Bunyan's concept of the covenant scheme coincided with that of the strict Calvinists and Antinomians.

In *The Doctrine of the Law and Grace Unfolded* Bunyan asserted that sinners were "brought into" the covenant of grace, and by this he implied that the covenant was made by God alone (or, more accurately, between the Father and the Son), without any real participation on man's part. Man could be said to covenant with God, but only in the sense that the Son, as man's "head and undertaker", covenanted for him. Having said this, Bunyan was then able to argue, with respect to the conditions necessary to be brought into the covenant: "All the conditions . . . are already fulfilled for us by Jesus Christ, . . . every promise that is a new Covenant promise, if there be any condition in it, our undertaker hath accomplished that for us. . . ." Consequently, when he wrote of conditions in his treatise on the covenants, it was primarily in terms of the conditions required by the Father of the Son rather than those required by God of man. Nevertheless, Bunyan did admit that, with respect to man, "there be a condition [i.e., faith] commanded in the Gospel . . .", but he added the all-important qualification that "he that commands the condition, doth not leave his children to their own natural abilities, that in their own strength they should fulfill them; . . . but the same God that doth command that the condition be fulfilled, even he, doth help his children by his holy Spirit to fulfill the same condition. . . ."[22]

Here Bunyan was reminiscent of Luther, who had written in his commentary on Galatians that

> the promises of the law are conditionall, promising life, not freely, but to such as fulfill the law. . . . But the promises of the new Testament have no such condition joyned unto them, nor require any

thing of us, . . . but bring and give unto us freely forgivenesse of sinnes, grace, righteousnesse and life everlasting for Christs sake. . . .

While it may be Luther's influence being manifested at this point, the basic idea was not different from that of the strict Calvinists. Archbishop Ussher, for example, wrote that "the gift being most free on Gods part, nothing is required on mans part but the receiving of grace offered; which is done in those that are of capacity by Faith in Christ. . . ." Owen stated even more plainly that "the condition of the Covenant is not said to be required, but it is absolutely promised. . . ." The Antinomians were more extreme, agreeing with Tobias Crisp's idea that "in way of condition of the Covenant you must do nothing".[23]

The moderate Calvinists can be distinguished by their emphasis on the conditions of faith and repentance as, in a real sense, man's act. These men would not deny the impossibility of fulfilling such conditions apart from the aid of divine grace, yet their emphasis was at least as much on these conditions as man's act as on God's working them in man. John Preston had earlier made this quite clear:

> The condition that is required of vs, as part of the Couenant, is the doing of this, the action, the performance of these things, it is to repent, to serue the Lord in newnesse of life, but the ability by which we are able to performe these, is a part of the Couenant on the Lords part, to haue new hearts and new spirits [Ezek. xxxvi. 26], whereby we are able to repent, and to bring forth fruite worthy of amendment of life. . . .[24]

The Arminian John Goodwin stressed the necessity of *man's* fulfilling the conditions of the covenant,[25] thus completing again the continuum running from Antinomian to Arminian.

If, as Bunyan said in 1659, "all the conditions . . . are already fulfilled for us by Jesus Christ . . .", was the covenant of grace really a covenant at all? It was possible to admit candidly, as did the Antinomian Saltmarsh, that "it were good, that we did not

rest too much in the notion of a Covenant . . .", primarily because
such a notion, he argued, did not conform to the New Testament:
"Nor is it the way of a covenant that the Gospel uses, but rather
the promise, or grace, or salvation; for the Spirit uses the word
Covenant onely by way of allusion; and because the soul being
under the power of the spirit, doth it self contract and covenant
with God to obey, though God gives no life in such a way of a
covenant or obedience." Other writers were not as extreme,
although they too essentially redefined the term "covenant" as
it applied to the covenant of grace. Owen emphasised its promissory nature, while Thomas Goodwin, reflecting on the necessity
of Christ's death to confirm the covenant, preferred to term it a
"Testament". For his part, Bunyan did not hesitate to use the
term "covenant" when referring to the covenant of grace inasmuch as his emphasis was placed predominantly on sinners
being brought into this covenant as it was made between the
Father and the Son—and this was a covenant even in the strictest
legal sense of the term.[26]

Because, according to Bunyan, "all the conditions . . . are
already fulfilled for us by Jesus Christ . . .", it would therefore
follow that the covenant of grace could not be made with all of
mankind, but must be made with the elect alone, else all men
would believe. Thus he clearly stated that the "Covenant of free
and unchangeable Grace, [is] made over to those thus chosen"
(i.e., the elect). John vi. 37, as he expounded it, referred to the
gift of the elect which was "bestowed upon Christ when the
Covenant, the Eternal Covenant was made between them before
all worlds". The limitation of the covenant of grace to the elect
was something which Bunyan held in common with strict
Calvinists, and was diametrically opposed to the Arminian contention that "the Covenant [of grace] is made with all Men,
without exception of any. . . ." For the Arminian, of course, this
meant only that grace was offered equally to all men, not that all
men actually belonged to the covenant of grace. In effect, Baxter
said the same thing when he wrote that "this Covenant of Grace,
being a conditional pardon of all the world, is universal in the
tenor or sense of it; It is of all Mankind without exception that

Christ saith, If thou confess with thy mouth, and believe in thy heart, thou shalt be saved: No person antecedently is excluded in the world". Having said this, however, he made a crucial distinction between his position—that of moderate Calvinism—and that of the Arminians by limiting the "Absolute promise of the first grace" to the elect alone. Interestingly enough, the Antinomians are here closer to the moderate than to the strict Calvinists. Vavasor Powell stated quite plainly that "God tenders the Covenant of grace . . . to all Nations, and to every creature; and it is the minde of God, that every Messenger and Minister of his, should declare and publish this Covenant to all. . . ."[27]

If the covenant of grace was made with the elect alone, regardless of whether or not it was, technically, tendered to all men, and if baptism (especially as practised with infants) was the seal of the covenant, then grave problems were raised when the supposedly visible saints and members of the elect began to stray from the ways of holiness. A strict Calvinist could reject paedobaptism, particularly as the seal of the covenant of grace, and make no distinction between the absolute promise of grace and the covenant of grace itself, as did the Baptist John Tombes in his three polemical treatises on *Anti-Paedobaptism*. The alternative was to retain infant baptism as a seal of the covenant of grace, but draw a distinction, as did the Independent Samuel Petto, between those who were "really" in this covenant and those who were only "visibly" participants in it.[28] According to the moderate Calvinists, whose solution to this problem bears some relationship to New England's Half-way Covenant, nonbelievers could in a real sense be part of the covenant of grace by virtue of the fact that—because their parents were believers—they could be baptised into the covenant as infants, though the covenant promises were conditional upon their later repentance and faith.[29] What was a major point of controversy for Calvinists in the mid-seventeenth century posed no real problem for Bunyan at all. Because he attributed practically no significance to baptism, and because he did not have to defend a personal conviction of the validity of paedobaptism, he was not faced with the knotty problem of explaining why those who had been baptised as infants into the covenant of grace (which, after all, was made, according to the Calvinist, only with the elect) had now strayed so far from the Christian life. This meant, though, that for Bunyan water baptism could not then be a seal of the covenant of grace; in his thought baptism by the Holy Spirit was quite adequate.

For Bunyan not only was the covenant of grace made with the elect alone, but as it was made with them it was also "unchangeable". The unchangeable nature of the covenant meant not that it was everlasting only in the sense that it would never be superseded by another covenant, as Ball and Blake argued, nor that it was "everlasting . . . upon the supposition of my obedience, but upon the unchangeable purpose of God, and the efficacy of the obedience of Christ. . . ." "My sins", Bunyan wrote from experience, "break not the Covenant: but them notwithstanding, God's Covenant stands fast with him. . . ." Preston, on the other hand, implied that the covenant could be broken when he wrote that it is "neuer nullified, vntill thou hast chosen to thy selfe another husband, till thou hast taken to thy selfe another Lord". Baxter, while maintaining the idea of the "Absolute promise of the first grace" to the elect, nevertheless cautioned his readers that the conditions required to continue in the covenant of grace were faith, consent, repentance, obedience, and perseverance. For Bunyan, though, in *The Pilgrim's Progress* once "Good Will" had opened the gate and the burdened pilgrim had struggled "till he came at a place somewhat ascending; . . . [upon which] stood a Cross, and a little below in the bottom, a Sepulcher," his eternal destiny was certain—troubled though his temporal journey might be.[30]

For such a troubled traveller as well as for the dejected soul struggling through the Slough of Despond, there was only one question of supreme importance: "Which of these two Covenants art thou under, soul?" Realising that "unless the great God of his infinite grace and bounty, had voluntarily chosen me to be a vessel of mercy, though I should desire, and long, and labour untill my heart did break, no good could come of it", the perplexed individual would probably reply: "How can you tell you are Elected?" The reply of the seventeenth-century preacher was almost invariably the same—faith, repentance, and acceptance of the promises—although the manner in which it was expressed naturally differed with each preacher. Bunyan himself stressed a personal, experiential awareness of being under the covenant of grace—and gave simple directions to achieve this otherwise elusive awareness:

> If thou wouldest . . . wash thy face clean, first take a glass and see where it is durty [*sic*]; . . . labour first to see them [i.e., your sins] in the glass of the Law. . . . Reckon thy self therefore, I say, the biggest sinner in the world, and be perswaded that there is none worse then thy self; then let the guilt of it seize on thy heart, then also go in that case and condition to Jesus Christ, and plunge thy self into his Merits, and the vertue of his Blood; and after that thou shalt speak of the things of the Law, and of the Gospel, experimentally. . . .

For those who still doubted, "the way to prove our selves under Grace" is, "by believing in Jesus Christ, . . . [to] triumph over the Devil, Sin, Death, and Hell. . . ."[31]

The Covenant of Grace: The Legal Aspect

> THEN he took him by the hand, and led him into a very large Parlour that was full of dust, because never swept; the which, after he had reviewed a little while, the Interpreter called for a man to sweep: Now when he began to sweep, the dust began so abundantly to fly about, that Christian had almost therewith been choaked: Then said the Interpreter to a Damsel that stood by, Bring hither Water, and sprinkle the Room; which when she had done, was swept and cleansed with pleasure.
>
> . . . This Parlor is the heart of a Man that was never sanctified by the sweet Grace of the Gospel: The dust, is his Original Sin, and inward Corruptions . . .; He that began to sweep at first, is the Law; but She that brought water, and did sprinkle it, is the Gospel. . . .
>
> Emmanuel Prince of Peace, and a great lover of the Town of Mansoul, I do . . . give them the holy Law, and my Testament, with all that therein is contained, for their everlasting comfort and consolation.[32]

These allegorical extracts point to, but do not solve, one of the most vexing questions which Bunyan and his contemporaries faced—the relation of law to the covenant of grace. Was Mansoul merely given back its old broom, or did Emmanuel give it a new one? In any case, of what use was a broom when there was no dust to be swept? Or, if there was dust to be swept, of what use was a broom which previously had raised only clouds of choking dust?

The legal aspect of the covenant of grace, according to Bunyan, involved believers only, for nonbelievers remained under the law as it was a covenant of works. The sinner "only and wholly standeth under the Law, as it is given in Fire, in Smoak, in Blackness, and Darkness, and Thunder; all which threaten him with Eternal ruin if he fulfil not the utmost tittle thereof. . . ." Luther had similarly admonished his readers: "He that setteth forth the law and workes to the old man, and the promise of forgivenesse of sinnes, and Gods mercy to the new man, devideth [*sic*] the word well."[33] This was also the position advocated by both the Antinomians and the strict Calvinists,[34] and was contrary to the contention of the Arminians and the moderate Calvinists that all men were now judged according to the covenant (or law) of grace.[35]

That all men are under two covenants, that of works or that of grace, was the premise of Bunyan's treatise, *The Doctrine of the Law and Grace Unfolded*. From this premise he deduced two "doctrines", the proof of which comprised the body of the treatise itself:

> First, that there are some in Gospel times, that are under the Covenant of Works.
> Secondly, that there is never a Believer under the Law, (as it is a Covenant of Works), but under Grace through Christ. . . .[36]

From the outset, then, Bunyan was careful to qualify Paul's oft-quoted dictum in Romans vi. 14, that believers "are not under the law, but under grace", with the phrase, "as it is a Covenant of Works". By making such a qualification at the very beginning of his treatise, Bunyan did not exclude the possibility that the covenant of grace may, as far as believers are concerned, have a legal aspect.

When Paul wrote that believers were no longer under the law, he meant, said Bunyan, that "you are not held, kept, or shut up by it, so as to appear before God under that administration, and none but that; or thus, you are not now bound by the authority of the Law, to fulfil it, and obey it, so as to have no salvation without you so do, or thus; if you transgress against any one tittle of it, you by the power of it must be condemned. . . ." To be freed from the law as it was a covenant of works meant release from the curse of the law for disobedience and from the necessity to seek righteousness for justification. "The Christian hath now nothing to do with the Law, as it thundereth and burneth on Sinai, or as it bindeth the conscience to wrath and the displeasure of God for Sin. . . ." To this extent, according to Bunyan, the believer was truly not under the law, but under grace.[37]

The basis of such statements—derived as they ultimately were from Pauline thought—was Bunyan's belief that the covenant of grace "'tis set in opposition" to the covenant of works. This, however, did not mean that the gospel and the law were "diametrically opposite one to another", which would logically result in unmitigated Antinomianism. Even the Antinomian Tobias Crisp acknowledged that the "Natures [of the law and gospel] are not so contrary, considering the true use the Law was intended for [Gal. iii. 19], but they may well agree together. . . ." Such a position was strikingly similar to Burgess' colourful statement that "the Law and the Gospel are not to be severed, but they mutually put a fresh relish and taste upon each other". In this light it is possible to understand Bunyan speaking of the Christian life as one governed by the "Law of Grace", a phrase associated in this period more characteristically with Baxter. Referring to I Corinthians ix. 21, Bunyan was mindful that the saint was "not without Law to God, but under the Law to Christ".[38]

To the difficulty in determining the precise nature of this law of Christ can be traced many of the questions which arose in the Antinomian controversy. The preacher who conceived of the law of Christ in terms of something basically spiritual or perhaps even mystical inevitably reached different conclusions about the place of law in the covenant of grace from those reached by the preacher who closely associated it with the moral law. The tendency of some Independent ministers to disparage the place of the moral law in the covenant of grace (and one recalls here Baxter's observation that "the Antinomians were commonly Independents") arose not from any desire to permit licentious and riotous behaviour, but rather because they "took the biblical demand for holiness so seriously as to limit Church membership to those whom they called 'visible saints', and then, in order to protect such Church members from the besetting sin of self-righteousness, made as large a distinction as might be between justification and sanctification".[39]

Few in the seventeenth century outdid Bunyan in his emphasis on justification *sola fide*, as expressed, for example, in his *Defence of the Doctrine of Iustification, by Faith in Jesus Christ* (1672) and *Of Justification by an Imputed Righteousness* (published in 1692), yet Bunyan was as fervent in his emphasis on sanctification—the holy life— as was such a staunch proponent of the legal nature of the covenant of grace as Baxter. "The Doctrine of the New Covenant", Bunyan wrote, "doth call for holiness, engage to holiness, and maketh the Children of that Covenant to take pleasure therein. Let no man therefore conclude . . . that the Doctrine of the Gospel is a licentious Doctrine. . . ." Bunyan was simply underscoring here the basic truth of Preston's earlier maxim that "he that beleeues in the greatest degree the promises of pardon and remission, I dare boldly say, he hath the holiest heart, and the holiest life. . . ." Such a holy life was a life lived according to the moral law; hence in *The Holy War* Emmanuel counselled Mansoul to "make thy self by my Law straight steps for thy feet. . . ."[40]

The "matter" of the moral law, which Bunyan defined in terms of Mark xii. 29–31, was not abrogated for the believer, for "without it he cannot be a rational creature. . . ." As it was delivered by Moses, however, the law ceased to exercise authority over those in the covenant of grace: "The ministration of it from Sinai, with the Circumstances belonging to that ministration, they are not Moral, not Everlasting, but Shadowish and Figurative onely." Here one is reminded of the words of George Fox, reflecting as they do the Antinomian tendencies of the Quakers: "I shewed y^m ye types & figures & shadowes of Christ in ye time of ye law & shewed y^m how y^t Christ was come y^t ended ye types & shadows & tyths & oaths & denyed swearinge & sett uppe . . . a free teachinge. . . ." Bunyan would not, however, go as far as to advocate the establishment of such "a free teachinge", for he drew a definite distinction between "the morality of the Law", from which believers were not exempt, and "the ministration of it upon Sinai", which ceased when Christ established the law of grace.[41] In denying the authority of the Mosaic law to bind believers, Bunyan was advocating the position of the strict Calvinists and the Antinomians.[42] Bunyan's position was rejected by Anthony Burgess, who specifically objected against "the Antinomian distinction of the Law abolished as a Law, but still abiding in respect of the matter of it. . . ." Blake argued that God maintained his sovereignty over the believer "in keeping up his commandments, the power and vigour of his precepts", and that the law continued to have a commanding power over those in the covenant of grace. Or, to put it bluntly, "the Law bindes [believers], as delivered by Moses". Trying, as always, to find a conciliatory position, Baxter once again straddled the theological fence by suggesting that "the Decalogue is materially in force, but not formally as part of the proper Mosaical Law. . . ."[43]

That which distinguished Bunyan as well as other strict Calvinists from those of an Antinomian persuasion was basically a matter of emphasis. Bunyan was careful to note that, in spite of the freedom of the believer from the law for his justification (which had been one of the favourite themes of Luther in his commentary on Galatians), "that Law be a rule for every one that believeth to walke by. . . ." Although an Antinomian preacher such as Walter Cradock might likewise recognise that "the substance and matter of the law" are "eternall, and a rule for all Saints . . .", the same preacher was more concerned that "when we were grown to full yeares, as we are under the Gospel, the Lord Jesus hath broken and dissolved those little childish lawes, those beggerly Rudiments: those A.B.C. lawes and accidences [*sic*] were for children". Another good example of such writing appeared in the writings of Saltmarsh, and provided a distinct contrast with Bunyan's position:

> Though the Law be a beam of Christ in substance and matter, yet we are not to live by the light of one beam now when the Sun of righteousnesse is risen himself. . . . What need we light up a Candle for the children of the day to see by? . . . Nor doth it become the glory of Christ revealed, to be beholding to any of the light upon Moses face.

Such statements were in definite contrast to Bunyan's references to the law as "a rule, or directory", and "a Rule of life" for those in the covenant of grace. His respect for the law was evident in his belief that a holy life was one which must be lived "according to the rule of holiness, the law. . . ."[44]

Nevertheless Bunyan did show some affinity with the Antinomians when he persistently referred to the law of grace as a "new Law".[45] There was, however, a scriptural basis (Rom. viii. 1) for such an affirmation, so that Bunyan could, with biblical precedent, assert that "the Child of God has sinned, and . . . there is a Law that condemneth for this Sin: But here is the thing, this Child is removed by an Act of Grace into, and under another Law". Crisp similarly contended that although a believer "do Sin, the Law hath no more to say to him then if he had not sin[n]ed", but unlike Bunyan, he did not qualify such a radical statement by indicating that the believer was nevertheless subject to the new law of Christ. Bunyan acknowledged the spiritual nature of this new law of grace when he wrote that it was "written and preserv'd" in "the Heart spiritual," but he did not draw Saltmarsh's extreme conclusion that "the Spirit . . . makes him [i.e., the believer] the very Law of Commandments in himself, and his heart the very two Tables of Moses. . . ." "The spiritual man", Saltmarsh elsewhere wrote, "who lives in the Spirit, is not under the meer law of the letter, but it is according to its spirituality, the principle and spirituall life of him. . . ." For Bunyan, on the contrary, the law might be said to be both new and spiritual, but it was never divorced from the moral law or a sense of objectivity: "The whole Law, as to the morality of it, is delivered into the hand of Christ, who imposes it now . . . as a Rule of life to those that have believed in him. . . ."[46]

Even though the Christian was now subject to a new law of grace, and though the law as it was delivered by Moses no longer had any binding power on him, the Mosaic law still had a rightful, but rigidly restricted, place in the covenant of grace:

> When this Law with its Thundering threatnings doth attempt to lay hold on thy conscience, shut it out with a promise of grace. . . . If it will be content with being my informer, and so lovingly leave off to judge me, I will be content . . .; but otherwise, I being now made upright without it, and that too with that righteousness, which this Law speaks well of and approveth; I may not . . . make it my Saviour and Judg[e], nor suffer it to set up its government in my conscience; for by so doing I fall from Grace. . . .[47]

Subject to these limitations, there was, for Bunyan, a legal aspect to the covenant of grace with respect not only to the law of grace in Christ, but also to the Mosaic law.

In his development of the concept of the covenants, Bunyan took the *via media* between the moderate Calvinists on the one hand and the Antinomians on the other. His position was, on the whole, at one with strict Calvinists such as John Owen and Samuel Petto, with the principal exception of his rejection of the concept of the baptismal covenant. More than most writers Bunyan elaborated upon the idea of the covenant of grace as it was first established between the Father and the Son, and this in turn accounted for the emphasis which he placed on the conditions of this covenant being fulfilled for the elect by Christ. Although Bunyan regarded this covenant of grace as diametrically opposed to the covenant of works, of which the Mosaic law was a restatement, he refrained from the excesses of the Antinomians, and instead granted to the law—particularly the "matter" of it as it was imposed on believers by Christ as a rule of life—a place in the covenant of grace.

It was with respect to the relation between law and grace that the influence of Luther on Bunyan's concept of the covenants was most evident, though even in this regard such influence was almost as much a matter of motivation as it was of providing him with the theological material from which to formulate his doctrine. Essentially this was because Luther was in no sense even remotely a covenant theologian. Furthermore, Luther's pronouncements on law and grace in his commentary on Galatians were made predominantly in the context of the doctrine of justification rather than on the place of the law in the life of the justified believer. Yet it is more than coincidence that Bunyan's first treatise of theological importance, published as early as 1659, should be entitled *The Doctrine of the Law and Grace Unfolded*, echoing as it did the theme of Luther's commentary: "The doctrine of grace can by no meanes stand with the doctrine of the law."[48] Although Bunyan's actual "unfolding" of the doctrines of law and grace evinced more Calvinist than Lutheran influence, the impression left on him by the reading of Luther's commentary was significant if for no other reason than that it created in him an intense interest in the role of law and grace in the salvation of the sinner—which in his day was expressed in terms of covenant theology.

NOTES

1. XII, p. 143.
2. XXIX, pp. 21–22.
3. XII, p. 8; XLV, pp. 11, 67; VIII, p. 56.
4. XII, fol. B1 *verso* and pp. 15, 43.
5. L, p. 191.
6. Cf. Baxter, *An End of Doctrinal Controversies* (1691), p. 134; John Ball, *A Treatise of the Covenant of Grace* (1645), pp. 93, 111; Anthony Burgess, *Vindiciae Legis* (2nd ed., 1647), pp. 213, 232–33; Thomas Blake, *Vindiciae Foederis* (1653), pp. 166–68; Samuel

Rutherford, *The Covenant of Life Opened* (Edinburgh, 1655), pp. 6off.

7. Cf. Owen, *The Branch of the Lord* (Edinburgh, 1650), p. 16; Saltmarsh, *Free-Grace*, pp. 167–68; Crisp, *Christ Exalted*, II, 246; Powell, *Christ and Moses*, p. 26; J. Goodwin, *Romans*, p. 103.

8. XXXIV, pp. 128–29; Luther, *Galathians*, fol. 153 verso; XXII, p. 51; XXIX, pp. 21–22.

9. XL, p. 17; Luther, *Galathians*, fol. 172 verso. Cf. John Preston, *The New Covenant* (1629), pt. 2, p. 148; T. Goodwin, *Works*, IV, pt. 3, p. 38; Saltmarsh, *Free-Grace*, p. 159; Powell, *Christ and Moses*, pp. 191ff. Ball, however, like Bunyan interprets this verse as a reference to the ceremonial law. *Covenant of Grace*, pp. 139ff.

10. III, p. 42.

11. XXII, pp. 36–38.

12. XLV, p. 65; Trinterud, "The Origins of Puritanism," *Church History*, XX (March, 1951), 54.

13. XII, p. 271; XLV, p. 66.

14. Cf. E. F., *The Marrow of Modern Divinity* (1645), p. 37; Saltmarsh, *Free-Grace*, p. 126; Crisp, *Christ Exalted*, I, 74ff.

15. Cf. Saltmarsh, *Free-Grace*, pp. 125–27; Powell, *Christ and Moses*, pp. 4ff.; Crisp, *Christ Exalted*, I, 8off.; Owen, *Branch of the Lord*, p. 17; Samuel Petto, *The Difference between the Old and New Covenant* (1674), pp. 19–21; T. Goodwin, *Works*, I, pt. 1, p. 63.

16. J. Goodwin, *Redemption Redeemed*, p. 458.

17. Baxter, *Doctrinal Controversies*, p. 121; and *Catholick Theologie*, Bk. I, pt. 2, chap. xxxviii; Rutherford, *Covenant of Life*, pp. 308ff.; Blake, *Vindiciae Foederis*, pp. 10–11, 24–25; XII, p. 133.

18. XXVIII, pp. 12–14.

19. Baxter, *Plain Scripture Proof of Infants Church-Membership and Baptism* (1651), p. 225. Cf. Preston, *New Covenant*, pt. 2, p. 70; Ball, *Covenant of Grace*, pp. 14–15; and Stephen Geree, *The Doctrine of the Antinomians by Evidence of Gods Truth Plainly Confuted* (1644), pp. 72–73.

20. Ussher, *Body of Divinitie*, p. 158; Owen, *Justification by Faith*, pp. 269–70. Cf. Petto, *Old and New Covenant*, p. 2; Saltmarsh, *Free-Grace*, pp. 125–26; Powell, *Christ and Moses*, pp. 20–21; Crisp, *Christ Exalted*, II, 255.

21. XLV, p. 67.

22. XII, pp. 222, 132, 275, 142–47, 115–16.

23. Luther, *Galathians*, fol. 218; Ussher, *Body of Divinitie*, p. 159; Owen, *Salus Electorum*, p. 103; Crisp, *Christ Exalted*, I, 83
24 Preston, *New Covenant*, pt. 2, p. 143. Cf. Baxter, *Doctrinal Controversies*, p. 142; Ball, *Covenant of Grace*, p. 17; Blake, *Vindiciae Foederis*, pp. 26–28; Geree, *Doctrine of the Antinomians*, pp. 72–74.
25. J. Goodwin, *Redemption Redeemed*, pp. 456, 458.
26. XII, p. 275; Saltmarsh, *Free-Grace*, p. 153; Owen, *Salus Electorum*, p. 103; T. Goodwin, *Works*, I, pt. 1, p. 396; XII, pp. 222ff.
27. XII, p. 275; XLII, p. 43; VII, p. 19; J. Goodwin, *Redemption Redeemed*, p. 457; Baxter, *Catholick Theologie*, Bk. I, pt. 2, chap. lxxvi; and *Plain Scripture Proof*, p. 225; Powell, *Christ and Moses*, p. 159.
28. Petto, *Old and New Covenant*, p. 262.
29. Cf. Baxter, *Plain Scripture Proof*, pp. 224, 226, 326; Ball, *Covenant of Grace*, pp. 24–25; Blake, *Vindiciae Foederis*, p. 20; Rutherford, *Covenant of Life*, pp. 72ff.
30. XLII, p. 43; Ball, *Covenant of Grace*, p. 23; Blake, *Vindiciae Foederis*, pp. 29–30; XXXIX, p. 60; XLIII, p. 395; Preston, *New Covenant*, pt. 2, p. 215; Baxter, *Plain Scripture Proof*, p. 225; and *Doctrinal Controversies*, p. 142; XXVIII, pp. 14, 35. For other strict Calvinist and Antinomian statements of the unchangeability of the covenant, see Petto, *Old and New Covenant*, pp. 66–67; Powell, *Christ and Moses*, pp. 74ff.; Crisp, *Christ Exalted*, I, 81.
31. XII, pp. 291–92; XVI, sect. 47; XII, fols. A5 verso–A6 and p. 146.
32. XXVIII, pp. 20–21; XXII, p. 214.
33. L, p. 191; Luther, *Galathians*, fol. 6 verso.
34. Cf. Powell, *Christ and Moses*, p. 207; Walter Cradock, *Mount Sion, or, the Priviledge and Practice of the Saints* (1649), ad cal. *Gospel-Holinesse* (1651), p. 209; Owen, *Sin and Grace*, p. 94; E.F., *The Marrow*, pp. 20–21; Rutherford, *Covenant of Life*, p. 14.
35. J. Goodwin, *et al.*, *Agreement*, p. 60; Baxter, *Doctrinal Controversies*, pp. 131, 151–52.
36. XII, pp. 4–5.
37. XII, p. 3; L, p. 191.
38. LVI, p. 565; LIII, p. 424; Crisp, *Christ Exalted*, IV, 91; Burgess, *Vindiciae Legis*, p. 153; XLII, p. 105; Baxter, *Catholick Theologie*, Bk. I, pt. 2, p. 22, and chap. lx; L, p. 191.
39. *Reliquiae Baxterianae*, Bk. I, pt. 1, sect. 162 (p. 111); Nuttall, *The Welsh Saints 1640–1660* (Cardiff, 1957), p. 32.
40. XII, p. 345; Preston, *New Covenant*, pt. 2, p. 103; XXII, p. 393.

41. XXXIII, p. 34; Fox, *Journal* (1911 ed.), I, 256; XXXIII, p. 37.
42. Cf. E.F., *The Marrow,* pp. 119–20; Owen, *Person of Christ,* p. 161; Powell, *Christ and Moses,* pp. 236ff.; Saltmarsh, *Free-Grace,* pp. 146 160.
43. Burgess, *Vindiciae Legis,* p. 214; Blake, *Vindiciae Foederis,* pp. 48–49, 56 (marginal reading); Baxter, *Catholick Theologie,* Bk. I, pt. 2, chap. xxxiii.
44. XL, p. 15; Cradock, *Mount Sion,* p. 218; and *Gospel-Libertie* (1648), p. 18; Saltmarsh, *Free-Grace,* pp. 146–47; L, p. 191; XXXIII, p. 38; XLVI, p. 223.
45. XXXIII, p. 36; XLII, p. 132; XXII, p. 131. Cf. Powell, *Christ and Moses,* p. 223; Saltmarsh, *Free-Grace,* pp. 146ff.; Cradock, *Gospel-Libertie,* p. 36. The usual Calvinist position was to make a distinction between "the Moral Preceptive Part" of the law, with respect to which "Christ gave no New Law " and "the Institutions of worship " which Christ abolished and in their place "gave a New Law of worship. . . ." Owen, *Person of Christ,* pp. 158–60.
46. XLII, pp. 103–104; Crisp, *Christ Exalted,* I, 123; XXXIII, p. 35; Saltmarsh, *Free-Grace,* p. 146; and *Sparkles of Glory* (1647), pp. 240–41; XXXIII, p. 38.
47. L, p. 191. Cf. Powell, *Christ and Moses,* p. 222; and Luther, *Galathians,* fols. 156–156 *verso.*
48. *Galathians,* fol. 30 *verso.*

5 The Pilgrim's Stately Palace

PILGRIMS MAKING THE ARDUOUS JOURNEY from the City of Destruction to the abode of eternal bliss were provided with a place of relief and security which Bunyan allegorically described as a "very stately Palace . . ., the name whereof was Beautiful, and it stood just by the High-way side". The palace, as he depicted it, was in reality the Separatist church, that exclusive and elite organisation in which godliness rather than wealth or social status or residence was the determining factor for membership. Those who comprised this special society had been required to manifest visible signs of election and participation in the covenant of grace. As far as other believers were concerned, each member had to demonstrate, both initially and continually, visible proof that he had embarked on the soteriological journey of the Christian pilgrim. Once a member of that society, he was expected to follow the spiritual leadership of the congregationally-chosen minister. Whether or not baptism was required as a condition of membership in this society varied with different churches, though all practised the sacrament of the Lord's supper and all emphasised an active life characterised by adherence to Christian principles.

The Church

HE [i.e., Christian] lift[ed] up his eyes, and behold there was a very stately Palace before him, the name whereof was Beautiful, and it stood just by the High-way side.

> So I saw in my Dream, that he made haste and went forward, that if possible he might get Lodging there. . . .

> Then said Christian to the Porter, Sir, What house is this? and may I lodge here to-night? The Porter answered, This House was built by the Lord of the Hill: and he built it for the relief and security of Pilgrims. . . .

> Por. Well, I will call out one of the Virgins of this place, who will, if she likes your talk, bring you in to the rest of the Family, according to the Rules of the House. So Watchful the Porter rang a Bell, at the sound of which, came out at the door of the House, a Grave and Beautiful Damsel, named Discretion. . . .[1]

Bunyan's concept of the church was based on the distinction between the invisible universal church, known only to God, and the visible particular church. The universal church, as Bunyan defined it, "comprehendeth all the Parts of it, even from Adam to the very Worlds end, whether in Heaven or Earth . . .", and "cannot be visible; a great Part of that vast Body being already in Heaven, and a great Part as yet (perhaps) unborn". In traditional terminology this was to define the universal church as the totality of the elect: "Christ's true Spouse is not to be a grain more, nor a dram less, but Just the number of God's Elect." A further distinction was made by Bunyan with respect to the universal church in terms of the earth-bound church militant and the heavenly church triumphant, though the fundamental unity of the church militant and the church triumphant was distinctly affirmed. At the same time, however, Bunyan warned that it was necessary to distinguish between the church militant as a part of the universal church and a "particular Congregation of professing Christians", which could, in spite of rigid entrance examinations, embody false professors.[2]

For Bunyan the church was a means of grace to the extent that it was "the place in which God doth beget all those that are the Children of his. . . . The Children of the Church are Heaven-born, begotten of God, and brought forth in the Church of Christ. . . ." As he wrote in his *Discourse . . . of the House of God:*

Under the very Threshold of this place
Arise those goodly springs of lasting grace,
Whose Christal [*sic*] Streams minister Life to those
That here of Love to her, make their repose. . . .

The importance of the church as a means of grace, however, was not any role it might have had in the initial conversion of the sinner, but rather the part it played in their subsequent growth in grace. "In the New Creation, Men spring not up by Nature to be Saints: No, not in the Church of God, but first they are created in Christ Jesus, and made meet to be Partakers of the Benefit, and then planted in the Church of God: planted, I say, as Plants before prepared." The church, in effect, was a garden—the soil in which the elect were planted and cultivated by the Master Gardener. Bunyan made this quite explicit, giving what he believed to be the divine reason for adopting such a course of action. That reason revealed Bunyan's paramount concern with the primacy of God in salvation: "The reason why Men by Nature grow not in the Church, is, because the Lord doth not cause it to rain upon them, they still abiding and doing according to the course of this World; but he plants them in his House by the mighty power of his Word and Spirit, by which they are created Saints, and then they afterwards grow in Grace. . . ." In a very real sense, therefore, it was true that for Bunyan *extra ecclesiam nulla salus*, since all the elect were planted by God in this ecclesiastical garden. In affirming this belief Bunyan reflected a Cyprianic passage found in Arthur Dent's *The Plaine Mans Path-Way to Heauen*. Dent reiterated traditional dogma when he asserted that "not one without the Church sh[o]uld be saued. For he that hath not the Church for his mother, cannot haue God for his Father."[3] At a very impressionable point early in his religious development that concept had influenced Bunyan.

It was not merely in the universal church that the elect were planted, but in the particular church as well. The nature of this church as it was viewed not only by Bunyan and his Bedford congregation but also by virtually all Independents and Baptists, had, as demonstrated by Geoffrey Nuttall, four basic principles:

It was to be (i) separated from the world (ii) as a fellowship of believers which was (iii) gathered together in freedom (iv) to live a life of holiness.[4]

That the church was to be separate from the world, including the parish churches which had succumbed to the encroachments of that world, was a principle which had been accepted by the Bedford congregation prior to Bunyan's becoming a member of it. With reference to the original formation of the church by John Gifford in 1650, a complaint was made that "the more antient professors, being used to live . . . wthout regard to such separate, and close comūnion, were not at first so ready to fall into that godly order". Yet eventually "they began to come to some blessed resolution therein", and the principle of separation was established in the life of the Bedford church.[5] Apparently the members of that church saw no contradiction in their Separatist position and simultaneous membership in a state church, for in 1653 Gifford was presented to the living of the parish church of St. John's at Bedford, and his little group of Separatists consequently became a part of the Cromwellian state church. Following Gifford's death in 1655, John Burton became rector of the church, a position which he held until his death in 1660. Shortly after his death the church was deprived of its use of St. John's by the restoration of the parish church to the Anglicans in conjunction with the reestablishment of the monarchy.

When, on 21 January, 1672, the "full assembly of the Church at Bedford . . . did at this meeting with joynt consent (signifyed by solemne lifting up of their hands) call forth and appoint our bro: John Bunyan to the pastorall office, or eldership", the problem of a possible association with the state church had been dead for twelve years. Thus Bunyan was able to enunciate the principle of separation without compromising that principle by the obligations imposed by being a part of a state church. As he wrote in his commentary on Genesis i–xi, published posthumously in 1692:

The work of the Church of God, is not to fall in with any sinful Fellowship, or receive into their Communion the ungodly World, but to shew forth the praises and vertues of him who hath called them out from among such Communicants into his marvellous Light.

Those admitted to church membership, according to Bunyan, were those who were "for separating from the unconverted and open prophane, and for building up one another an holy Temple in the Lord, through the Spirit".[6]

In *The Pilgrim's Progress*, once Christian had approached the Palace entrance and requested admission, the Porter called for

> one of the Virgins of this place, who will, if she likes your talk, bring you in to the rest of the Family, according to the Rules of the House. So Watchful the Porter rang a Bell, at the sound of which, came out at the door of the House, a Grave and Beautiful Damsel, named Discretion. . . .

This was the principle of separation in operation, for it was the task of Discretion to determine whether or not the inquirer was serious in his intent to separate from the world. This was no mere theological dictum dressed in allegorical fancy; it was hard fact for the seventeenth century Separatist. A look at the procedure established for accepting new members into the Bedford church will establish this:

> We do also agree that such persons as desire to joyne in fellowship, if upon the conference of our friends with them, who shall be sent for that purpose; our saide friends be satisfyed of the truth of the worke of grace in their heartes; then they shall desire them to come to the next church-meeting, and to waite neare the place assigned for the meeting, that they may be called in. . . . But if the brethren sent forth, be not satisfyed in, the worke of Grace in the persons they are sent to; then they shall not desire their coming to ye Church meetinge.[7]

A careful reading of the records of the Separatist churches in the seventeenth century will illustrate the common use of this procedure.

The principle of fellowship had also been clearly established when the Bedford church was formed, for the members had "determined to walke together in the fellowship of the Gospell. . . ." Consequently, "after prayer, and seeking God as before; wth one consent they joyntly first gave themselves to the Lord; and one to another by the will of God." Very similar is article xxxiii of the confession of faith issued by the Particular Baptists in London in 1644, which stated that the members of a church were "joyned to the Lord, and each other, by mutuall agreement. . . ." Bunyan himself, when defining the word "Communion", wrote: "I mean fellowship in the things of the Kingdom of Christ, or that which is commonly called Church Communion, the Communion of Saints."[8] A reading of the records of the Bedford church frequently reveals notations of persons "received to walke in fellowship with this Congregation". To be a member of a Separatist church was to belong to this fellowship or communion of saints; it was with this fellowship in mind that John Owen wrote his *Eshcol: . . . or Rules of Direction, for the Walking of the Saints in Fellowship according to the Order of the Gospel* (1648).

The third principle—that of freedom—also found expression from the very first in the Bedford church. Compulsion in religion, especially the forcing of individuals to attend their parish church, was repudiated in favour of the freedom to gather together, or rather to be gathered together by God, to worship. Hence *The Church Book*, under the heading of "A Brief account of the 1st Gathering of the Church of Christ at Bedford", recorded the efforts of Gifford "to gather into Gospell-fellowship, the saintes, and brethren, in and about this towne. . . ." This principle was practised so effectively that shortly after Bunyan was appointed pastor of the church it was holding meetings in and accepting members from a place as distant as Gamlingay, Cambridgeshire. In setting forth his rule for admission to church communion, Bunyan defined it as "that Rule by which they are discovered to the Church to be visible Saints; and *willing to be gathered* into their Body and Fellowship". The freedom of the gathered church was quite distinct from the central idea of the parish church, as enunciated by an opponent of the gathered church concept,

Richard Baxter: "Co-habitation is in Nature and Scripture Example, made the necessary Disposition of the Materials of a Church."[9]

In the Bedford church and in Bunyan's ecclesiology this freedom was manifested in yet another way. From its inception membership in the Bedford church required only "ffaith [sic] in Christ; & Holines[s] of life, without respect to this or that circumstance, or opinion in outward, and circumstantiall things". Bunyan himself later wrote that "Faith and Holiness, must be the Essentials, or Basis, upon, and for the sake of which you receive them. . . ." Baptism by water in any form was not a *sine qua non* of church membership. Bunyan expounded upon this theme at length in his *Confession of Faith*, affirming that he would have church communion with all visible saints, who "by the Word of the Gospel have been brought over to Faith and Holiness . . .", regardless of their views on the subject of baptism. To stipulate any conditions other than these for church membership was to require "things that are circumstantial. . . ." When he was verbally attacked for advocating this principle by Baptists Thomas Paul, William Kiffin, and John Denne, who asserted the necessity of believers' baptism for church communion, Bunyan replied with his *Differences in Judgment about Water-Baptism, No Bar to Communion* (1673). This freedom allowed by Bunyan and other like-minded men such as Henry Jessey, was no more acceptable to the paedobaptists than it was to most anti-paedobaptists. Yet throughout this particular controversy—and his ministry as a whole—Bunyan remained adamant in his belief that men were to be received into the church solely "by a Discovery of their Faith and Holiness, and their Declaration of Willingness to subject themselves to the Laws and Government of Christ in his Church".[10]

Freedom had its bounds, and consequently there was a point at which it was mandatory that the principle of holy fellowship limit the principle of freedom if the excesses of that freedom were not to destroy the church itself. Disciplinary measures were necessary if the fellowship and the holiness (the fourth principle) of the separated church were to be maintained. Referring to the snuffers which accompanied the candlesticks in Solomon's temple (I Kings vii. 50), Bunyan observed: "If our snuf[f]s are our superfluities of naughtiness; our Snuffers then are those righteous reproofs, rebukes, and admonitions, which Christ has ordained to be in his House [i.e., church] for good. . . ." This was no mere theory, for in 1674, for example, a Sister Landy was admonished, among other things, "for countenancing card-play. . . ." If, as in the case of Edward Dent in 1677, such admonition was insufficient to produce reformation, recourse was had to the congregationally administered ban. The step was a serious one, and meant, in effect, pulling the weeds out of God's garden—an open pronouncement to the world that the excommunicated person was judged not to be a recipient of divine electing grace. This was the judgement of the congregation when, in 1673, John Rush was "cast out of the church . . . for he could not be carried home from the Swan to his own house without the help of no less than three persons, . . . he was so dead drunke." Similarly, in the same year "the wife of our Bro Witt" was cast out "for railling, and other wicked practises". In Bunyan's words this meant expulsion "by the holy compulsion of the Church . . . [and] by the Judicial Judgment of God. . . ."[11]

Expulsion by the congregation was a standard procedure of Baptists and Independents, working in all churches of these persuasions virtually as it did in the Bedford church. The Presbyterians, on the other hand, committed the power of admonition and excommunication solely to the officers of the church, in whose possession were "the Keys of the Kingdom of Heaven. . . ." Regardless of the method employed, there would have been sober agreement with this short verse of Bunyan's:

If he before the Church, repenteth not?
Deal with him as the matter shall require
Let not the House for him be set on fire.

Quite possibly Bunyan was here recalling the admonition of Lewis Bayly in *The Practise of Pietie*: "If Iustice requireth that one rather than vnitie must perish, and that a rotten member

must be cut off, to saue the whole body from putrifiing [*sic*];
fiat Iustitia."[12]

The fourth and perhaps the most important principle of the
church for Bunyan and for all Separatists was that of holiness:
"None [are] subjects of the visible Kingdom of Christ [or the
church] but visible Saints by Calling. . . ." The significance of
this position was not lost on the Separatists' contemporaries, for
Richard Baxter listed as one of the things which distinguished
the Independents from the Presbyterians the principle of requiring
as a "necessary Qualification of Church Members" that they be
visible saints. This was in 1655, but by 1689 with different conditions prevailing in the sphere of politico-religious relations,
Baxter acknowledged that "St. Paul wrote to no Church but such
as he called Saints; and I am sure Christ will save none but Saints:
An unsanctified Christian, and a Church not holy, are contra-
dictions *in adiecto*". It is, of course, possible to find such statements in the writings of most Christian authors. Archbishop
James Ussher wrote:

> God doth use outward measures with the inward, for the gathering
> of his Saints; and calleth them as well to outward profession among
> themselves, . . . whereby the Church becomes visible; hence it is
> that so many as partake of the outward meanes, and joyne with the
> Church in league of visible profession; are therefore in humane
> judgement accounted members of the true Church, and Saints by
> calling. . . .

In one sense, then, all churches were composed of visible saints,
but there was a real difference between those on the right, like
Ussher and Baxter, and those on the left, like Bunyan and his
fellow Separatists, even if it was a difference of emphasis. As
Geoffrey Nuttall wisely observed: "it was not . . . their underlying purpose which distinguished them so much as the strictness
with which in practice they interpreted the demand."[13]

Bunyan chose to interpret the demand for holiness most
strictly. The church must be holy, and this could be achieved
only if "the right and Gospel-Pattern" was followed, namely,

"that none be admitted into Church-Communion, but such who are visible Saints by Calling. . . ." To have communion with those who were not visible saints was to pollute the divine ordinances. Bunyan was aware, however, that even to limit church membership to visible saints would not mean that all church members were true believers.

> Now visible Church-Communion doth not absolutely call for onely invisible Saints, neither can it: for if the Church was to joyn with none but those whom they knew to be the very Elect of God (as all invisible Saints are) then she must joyn with none at all; for it is not possible that any Church should be so infallible to judge in that manner of the Elect, as to discern them always, and altogether from the non-Elect, which cannot be an invisible Saint.

The responsibility of the church was "to judge of Persons by their Words and Lives; they know not the Heart absolutely: and therefore if in Word and Life a man be as he ought, he is to be accounted a visible Saint, and orderly ought to be received of the Church as such. . . ."[14]

In order to maintain the principle of holiness in the church, there must be a "prescript Rule" regulating "the right to Ordinances, and the inlet into the Church. . . ." This rule by which prospective candidates were to be judged was no more and no less than "the Word of Faith, and of good Works, moral Duties Gospelized. . . ." That this rule was for the *esse* and not merely the *bene esse* of the church was evidenced by Bunyan's definition of the church as "one gathered or Constituted by, and walking after the Rule of the Word of God".[15] Such was the nature of the particular Palace in which every Separatist of Independent and Baptist persuasion sojourned on his pilgrimage to the eternal, universal Palace and the better life.

The Ministry

> I saw also that he looked this way, and that way, as if he would run; yet he stood still, because as I perceived, he could not tell which

way to go. I looked then, and saw a Man named Evangelist coming
to him, and asked, . . . why standest thou still? He answered,
Because I know not whither to go. . . .

Then said Evangelist, pointing with his finger over a very wide
Field, Do you see yonder Wicket-gate? The Man said, No. . . . Do
you see yonder shining light? He said, I think I do. Then said
Evangelist, Keep that light in your eye, and go up directly thereto,
so shalt thou see the Gate; at which when thou knockest, it shall
be told thee what thou shalt do.[16]

Thus did Bunyan describe the role of John Gifford in his own
conversion. Thereafter he maintained throughout his life a high
opinion of the ministry. Yet this respect never led him to formulate a sacerdotal theory of the ministry; his conviction was rather
that even as "the Temple [of Solomon] was higher then the
Pillars, . . . so is the Church then her Officers. . . ." The ministry
was not essential for the existence of the church, as conservatives
such as Baxter contended. The latter, for example, argued that if
there were no ministers, then there would be "no Church, no
Baptism, and then no Christ, and no Salvation". Bunyan, for his
part, had not the slightest intention to disparage the ministry,
though he did feel constrained (even as a minister) to caution
his readers not to be over dependent on ministers.[17]

Bunyan valued the ministry sufficiently to regard it as an important means of grace, but he also insisted upon the right of
each local congregation of visible saints to authorise a believer of
their choice to assume the duties of a minister. When the Bedford
congregation did "call forth and appoint our bro: John Bunyan
to the pastorall office, or eldership . . .," they were themselves in
effect a means of grace as the divine instrument used to appoint
a selected servant to special service. Once a minister had been
appointed in such a manner, it was his task "to make Sinners by
[his] preaching meet for the house of God". In his work the
minister had, so far as Bunyan was concerned, not only the sanc-
tion of his church but also the specific authority of God: "When
God ordained a word of grace to save us, he also in his Decree
provided Ministers to preach it to us to that end." It was by the

minister's proclamation of the word of grace that the elect were gathered together.

> The Distributor of the word of Grace
> He is, and at his Mouth, when he's in place,
> They seek the Law, he also bids them do it;
> He shews them Sin, and learns them to eschew it.[18]

Although the ministry was not sacerdotal, it certainly did not lack in Bunyan's thought either significance or a divine authority.

There were certain distinct qualifications which it was necessary for a minister to possess. He must be, said Bunyan, doctrinally sound, have the ability to teach, reprove, and exhort, be exemplary in faith and holiness, and be capable of calling the church together and directing its worship. To possess these abilities, however, did not necessarily mean that a minister was also himself the recipient of saving grace. Those ministers who did have both abilities and grace were such that "the profit of their gifts shall be rewarded by vertue of their grace . . .", but those who were not the subjects of electing grace, although part of the visible particular church, were not part of the universal church and hence would eventually be damned. They had still been divinely appointed to be servants in the church and were consequently means of grace, but they did not possess "the life, and power and saving operations of the justifying and preserving Grace of the Gospel. . . ."[19]

In spite of his divinely bestowed gifts the minister was (as in Pauline thought) fundamentally a servant. "Gifts make a Minister; and as a Minister, one is but a servant to hew Wood, and draw Water for the house of my God." According to the *Church Book,* after Bunyan was appointed pastor of the Bedford congregation, "he accepting thereof gave up himself to *serve* Christ, and his church in that charge. . . ." As a servant Bunyan's task could be summed up in terms of the conversion of sinners and the improvement of saints "by that measure of Perfection that God hath appointed on this side Glory. . . ." Bunyan likened the minister's work to that of a porter, "because as Porters stand at the Gate, and there open to, or shut upon those that make an attempt to enter in; so the Ministers of Christ by the Doctrine of the Twelve, do both open to, and shut the Gates against the Persons that will be attempting to enter in at the Gates of this City". In the last analysis, however, this power did not actually rest in the hands of ministers but of God, who alone "can let in souls into this City. . . . 'Tis not he and Saints together. . . ." The minister might be exalted to a place of service, but by himself he had no power except as he was a channel of divine grace and authority. Bunyan would have approved of Baxter's statement that ministers were believers' "Teachers, Fathers, and instructers under Christ, who are helpers of their joy, though they have not dominion over their Faith, and are Overseers, though not Lords and Owners of the Flock. . . ."[20] Such concepts were diametrically opposed to those which had characterised Laudian ecclesiological thought, and were indicative of the greater role allotted to the saints in the government of the church and even of the nation.

The Sacraments

TWO Sacraments I do believe there be,
Baptism and the Supper of the Lord:
Both Mysteries divine, which do to me,
By Gods appointment, benefit afford:
But shall they be my God? or shall I have
Of them so foul and impious a Thought,
To think that from the Curse they can me save?
Bread, Wine, nor Water me no ramsom [*sic*] bought.

This short poem was the most sacramental of all Bunyan's statements regarding baptism and the Lord's supper. These two ordinances—the term which he, like most Puritans and sectaries, preferred to use when referring to them—were, in fact, only two of a number of ordinances, which included prayer, church fellowship, the giving of alms, and the hearing and reading of Scripture.

Bunyan seemed intent to minimise any possible soteriological significance which might be attached to these ordinances, but without going to the extent of rejecting them entirely.

> I ... declare my reverent Esteem of them; yet dare not remove them, as some do, from the place, and end, where by God they are set and appointed; nor ascribe unto them more than they were ordered to have in their first and primitive Institution. . . .

In his controversy on the question of the necessity of baptism for church membership Bunyan charged his adversaries with attributing excessive importance to baptism, but he was careful to qualify his criticism of their position by stating that "I do not plead for a despising of Baptism, but a bearing with our Brother, that cannot do it for want of Light."[21]

On the one hand baptism and the Lord's supper were, for Bunyan, merely two of a number of ordinances, but on the other they were distinguished by virtue of the fact that they were the "shadowish, or figurative Ordinances". He explicitly warned his readers not to be satisfied with these "Shadowish Sacraments", but to rely only on faith. With the other ordinances the sacraments were means of grace only to the extent that the proper use of them brought increased knowledge of God and divine strength to enable the pilgrim better to serve God according to the moral law. Considered by themselves such sacraments were to be viewed as "Servants . . . and our Mystical Ministers, to teach and instruct us, in the most weighty Matters of the Kingdom of God . . .;" they were "Representations of the Death and Resurrection of Christ, and . . . as God shall make them Helps to our Faith therein. . . ."[22]

Both sacraments were regarded by Bunyan as means to God's presence by which pilgrims could "meet with God; and by them they are builded, and nourished up to Eternal life". Sacraments were divinely ordained "for men to travel and trade in, for the good and whol[e]some merchandize of Heaven, as the men of this world do for the things thereof, in the Streets and Open places of their Cities and places of priviledge". Although the sacraments were not to be regarded as fundamentals of the Christian faith, they were nevertheless useful in supporting one's faith, mortifying the desires of the earthly man, and strengthening believers to live in accordance with the moral law.[23]

Bunyan's concept of the sacraments was in the Zwinglian tradition, which had been propagated in England by the Elizabethan Separatist Robert Browne and which was also manifest, for example, in a confession of faith issued by the Particular Baptists of London in 1644. Such a concept was in contrast to the more widespread Calvinist interpretation of the sacraments as special means of saving grace. Bunyan himself went even further from the traditional position than Zwingli and Browne by refusing to associate closely the sacraments—particularly baptism—with the covenant of grace. Paedobaptists and anti-paedobaptists alike generally made such an association. Lewis Bayly for example, wrote: "We (in Baptisme) haue made a more speciall Couenant with God, to keepe his Commandements: and God hath couenanted with vs, to free vs from the Curse, and to assist vs with his spirit to keepe his Lawes." Baxter developed this theme at length in his writings. The Particular Baptist William Kiffin referred to baptism as "the solemn form of our Initiation into Covenant with God . . .", but Bunyan never found a place for such a concept in his own thought.[24]

In the baptismal controversy in which Bunyan was engaged with the Baptists in the 1670's, he insisted that baptism was not required for church membership. That insistence was grounded on his concept that baptism was essentially an insignificant ordinance, both in terms of church worship and in terms of doctrine. Baptism, Bunyan argued, was not given to the church as a law of worship by Christ, hence it was "no part of Church-worship as such. . . ." It concerned only individual pilgrims. To this rejection by Bunyan of baptism as a law of worship for the church, Danvers retorted: "It must either be an Ordinance left by Christ for the Church to manage and order, or to the World, for I know no medium. . . ." Danvers thus categorically rejected Bunyan's distinction between the individual and the society as the proper custodian of the baptismal ordinance. In a similar vein Thomas Paul argued that baptism was a foundation of the church with respect to its order, but Bunyan rejected this contention by asserting that the sole foundation of the church was Christ alone. Baptism had no place at all in the work of the church *qua* church. In fact, Bunyan concluded, it was not even essential for the *bene esse* of the church.[25]

Baptism was not, for Bunyan, "the initiating, and ent[e]ring Ordinance into Church Communion . . ."—what might be called "the Door of Entrance into the Church . . ."—because for him it did not grant membership to any church, either particular or universal. This was contrary to the usual Baptist position, according to which baptism was "an entrance and door into the Visible Church . . .", and the "Listing, Espousing, Covenanting, Ingrafting, Implanting Ordinance. . . ." Baxter alternatively argued that baptism admitted a believer to the universal but not the particular church.[26]

Bunyan's adversaries resorted to the argument that circumcision was the Old Testament type of baptism, and as such was, in the later words of Danvers, the "visible door of entrance into the Old testament-church, and so essentially necessary thereto, that without it none were esteemed either Church Members, or were to Partake either of the Passover, or of any of the Priviledges thereof. . . ." Bunyan, on the other hand, contended that "circumcision in the flesh, was a Type of Circumcision in the heart, and not of Water-baptism". "The Word of Faith and Holiness . . . is the Gospel Concision Knife . . . by which New-Testament Saints are circumcised in Heart, Ears, and Lips." The Welsh evangelist Vavasor Powell similarly felt that "circumcision in the flesh, did signifie the circumcision of the heart . . .", though he was also of the opinion that baptism was designated by Christ to take the place of circumcision. The Antinomian New Model Army chaplain John Saltmarsh, in much the same manner as Bunyan, rejected the idea that circumcision was a type of baptism inasmuch as "Baptisme [by water] is as a flash of lightning, . . . Circumcision [as a permanent mark on the body] was as a fixed Star. . . ."[27]

For Bunyan, then, baptism by water was not a prerequisite of church membership, and was not therefore to be made "a Wall of

Division between the Holy and the Holy: the Holy that are, and the Holy that are not so baptized with Water as we". The church must have communion with those with whom God would have communion, regardless of the type of their baptism or even their lack of it. Denne, however, objected to this assertion, contending that God had communion with many—such as children—with whom the church was not to have communion.[28]

Bunyan was willing to have communion with those of different convictions about baptism because of his basic conviction that love must prevail constantly over varying opinions on this issue. For Thomas Paul such a position was untenable on the grounds that "that man that makes affection the rule of his walking, rather then Judgement, it is no wonder to me, if he go out of the way". To this Bunyan replied: "Love to them we are perswaded that God hath received, is Love that is guided by Judgment; and to receive them that are such, because God hath bidden us (Rom. 14.) is Judgment guided by Rule." According to Kiffin this could not be love, for love could not be "exercised in opposition to the Order prescribed in the Word, by which Ordinances ought to be Administ[e]red. . . ." In the end the whole argument could be reduced to a question of whether or not love would triumph over ecclesiasticism, and Bunyan harboured no doubts about his preference for the former alternative.[29]

The great danger regarding baptism, according to Bunyan, was that it was often nothing but "an outward Conformity to an outward Circumstance in Religion. . . ." Even at best it was only one of a number of relatively superfluous "outward things". Bunyan was undoubtedly influenced in this aspect of his thought by his first pastor, John Gifford, who regarded baptism as one of the "externalls" of the Christian faith. Gifford and Bunyan were fairly close here to the Quaker position on the sacraments, as exemplified by George Fox's description of them as "temporall thinges", and his consequent advice to his followers to seek "y^t which cometh doune from above (& a feedeinge upon y^t & a feloweshippe in y^t) . . .", for "ye thinges y^t are not seene are eternall [II Cor. iv. 18]." Very likely an awareness of Bunyan's tendency toward this position prompted Denne's objection to

Bunyan's reference to baptism as something circumstantial; Denne instead asserted that it was "a Principle of the Doctrine of Christ, a Foundation-principle. . . ."[30]

Since baptism was, in Bunyan's thought, "an outward Circumstance", then those who prohibited communion because of differences about baptism were said to err in "a substance" whereas those who were not baptised erred only in "a circumstance". It was true, admitted Bunyan, that baptism was a duty of the believer, but it was neither an essential part of the Gospel nor a necessary prerequisite to church communion. Denne took precisely the opposite position, as did Danvers, who reasoned that "if it be prepostrous and wicked for a Man and Woman to cohabite together, and to enjoy the Priviledges of a Marriage-state, without the passing of that publick Solemnity; So it is no less disorderly upon a Scriptural account, for any to claim the Priviledges of a Church, or be admitted to the same till the passing of this Solemnity by them." The implication here was that if one had not experienced the sacrament of baptism, he could not properly be regarded as a Christian, even as one who had not gone through the wedding ceremony could not be truly married. Bunyan, though, completely rejected any soteriological significance for baptism: "A Failure in such a Circumstance as Water, doth not unchristian us. . . ." Denne hedged his position by suggesting that "although Baptism doth not make a Christian, yet the want of it may mar a Christian, and the neglect thereof unchristian men". Even more removed from Bunyan's position was the more sacramental view of a man such as Baxter, who stated simply that "Baptism doth but make us Christians. . . ."[31]

That which was of fundamental importance in the whole baptismal controversy, as far as Bunyan was concerned, was not the question of baptism's soteriological significance (or lack of it), but the more important concern that

I walk according to my Light with God: otherwise 'tis false [i.e. baptism is false]; For if a man that seeth it to be his Duty shall despisingly neglect it; or if he that hath no Faith therein shall foolishly take it up: both these are for this the worse, being convicted in themselves for Transgressors. He therefore that doth it according to his Light, doth well, and he that doth it not, or dare not do it for Want of Light, doth not ill. . . .

To this argument of Bunyan's, Thomas Paul posed the query: "Is it a Persons light, that gives being to a Precept?" Although Bunyan answered in the negative, he qualified his answer by observing that it was the believer's "Light and Faith about it, that can make him to do it acceptably". Denne made the same point as Thomas Paul, but in addition was quick to point out that Bunyan was here advocating the same basic principle for which he attacked the Quakers, namely, that the Light within was the rule by which Christians were to live. In Denne's opinion, "the question is not, who have Light therein, but who ought to have Light therein? . . ."[32]

Bunyan never felt compelled to deal with the question about the individual's responsibility for the presence or lack of light concerning baptism, since for him it was not man's place to question the sovereignty of God in his granting of more light to one man than to another. Therefore Bunyan could with Calvinist logic insist that a man was not to be refused communion in the church if his light differed from that of others. When Thomas Paul criticised him on this point for being "an Advocate for Sin against God, in the breach of One of his Holy Commands . . .", Bunyan retorted that "men must have Light, that they may not do in darkness, or Papist-like, live by an implicite Faith". A definite distinction must be maintained, Bunyan argued, between moral evil and "want of Light" with respect to baptism. In the end recourse must be had to the principle of freedom, for a Christian who was not "by Grace a Partaker of Light, in that Circumstance [baptism by water] which thou professest . . . is [yet] a Partaker of that Liberty and Mercy by which thou standest". On this basis Bunyan, in truly ecumenical fashion, rejected the argument of Baptists such as Thomas Paul that those baptised in infancy had to repent of that ceremony before being admitted to membership in a Baptist church.[33]

"Want of Light" with regard to baptism was, for Bunyan, an

essentially insignificant matter because it related to the practice
or ceremonial aspect of the ordinance rather than to its doctrinal
significance. The doctrinal significance of baptism he defined as
"that which by the outward Sign is presented to us, or which by
the outward Circumstance of the Act is preached to the Believer:
viz. The Death of Christ; My Death with Christ; also his Resurrection from the Dead, and mine with him to Newness of Life".
Because the Christian was dead to sin and alive to God, he already
possessed the power and doctrine of baptism, and if unbaptised
he consequently lacked only "the Sign, the Shadow, or the outward Circumstance thereof. . . ." But Bunyan's careful distinction
between the practice and the doctrine of baptism did not go
unchallenged. Thomas Paul immediately argued that it was very
unlikely that those who rejected baptism by water could have
"the Doctrine of Baptism", by which he meant "the Command,
that a believer ought to be baptized in Christ's Name, for such
ends which the Gospel expresses. . . ." Bunyan's retort made it
apparent that the real issue at this point centred around what
actually comprised the doctrine of baptism: "A man may preach
the Command, yet none of the Doctrine which Baptism preacheth.
The Doctrine lyeth not in the Command, but the mystery discovered to Faith, by the act." Once again Bunyan threw the issue
back to a matter of divine sovereignty, for if a right understanding
of the doctrine was dependent on faith, and if faith itself was in
turn dependent on prevenient grace, then who was man to
question God's acts?[34]

The important thing for every believer, as far as Bunyan was
concerned, was that he had the much more important baptism
of the Holy Spirit. In his stressing of the importance of Spirit
baptism along side of his relative disparaging of baptism by
water, Bunyan was closely akin to the Enthusiasts of his day.
John Saltmarsh, for example, had rejected baptism by water in
favour of baptism solely by the Holy Spirit: "I beleeve, that as
the Lord did suffer the Law of Ceremonies to dye out by degrees,
and to be worn out by the ministration of the Gospel, so he did
that part of Johns Ministery, of washing, by the Baptism of
Christ, of his Spirit. . . ."[35] This baptism of the Spirit was, of

course, also part of orthodox doctrine, but never to the exclusion of baptism by water. Baxter provided an idea of their relative significance even for the orthodox when he wrote that "it is not the meer Baptism of water, but the Baptism of the Holy Ghost which is given in Conversion, that maketh you living members of the Body".[36] It was this baptism of the Spirit which Bunyan saw discussed in Ephesians iv. 1–6 as the basis of church communion. Thus, in spite of his adversaries' protests that it was baptism by water which was referred to in Ephesians iv, Bunyan championed Spirit baptism as the only baptism requisite for membership in the church.

As far as baptism by water was concerned, Bunyan was thoroughly at one with his Baptist controversialists in affirming that the proper subjects of this sacrament were visible saints alone: "They only that have before received the Doctrine of the Gospel, and so shew it [to] us by their Confession of Faith, they only ought to be baptized." A man did not, according to Bunyan, become a visible saint as the result of baptism; he had to be one before he was baptised. Bunyan would not accept the more traditional view, as stated here by Baxter, that "Baptizing us is making us visible Christians, or the solemn entrance into the state of Christianity". This assertion came of course, from a staunch paedobaptist, but towards those of such a persuasion Bunyan was tolerant: although it was true that to be baptised "without Light going before" might be hypocritical, it was also true that believers were to bear with the "Infirmities" of those who regarded infant baptism as a duty. What might be designated Bunyan's rule of baptism was his belief that "when Persons can be baptized to their Edification, they have the liberty".[37]

The meaning of baptism for the visible saint who subjected himself to the ordinance was, for Bunyan, not only a strengthening of his faith in the death and resurrection of Christ and the concomitant understanding of his own death, burial and resurrection to a new life, but also a confirmation of the forgiveness of his sins. "He should know by that Circumstance, that he hath received Remission of Sins; if his Faith be as true, as his being baptized is felt by him." Baptism could thus be referred to as "the Symbol of Regeneration", a phrase commonly used by other writers, but ordinarily with greater import (by those who regarded the sacraments as primary means of grace) than Bunyan himself attributed to it. Baxter, for example, wrote: "Baptism is ordained to signifie and seal, and thereby confer remission of sins. . . ." This was far more sacramental than Bunyan ever was. A final meaning attached by Bunyan to baptism connected it to the holy life of the sanctified believer, for one of the primary "ends for which that appointment was Ordained . . ." was good works.[38]

Such was Bunyan's concept of the divisive sacrament of baptism. In his hands that doctrine received the kind of treatment which might have opened a path to Christian unity, at least as far as this issue was concerned. For a time he had a considerable following, but in the end the Baptists forgot Bunyan, and adhered to the position vigorously defended by his opponents in the baptismal controversy of the 1670's.

Bunyan had considerably less to say about the sacrament of the Lord's supper than he had about baptism. Discussion of this sacrament was not extensive in Puritan and Restoration England. Baptist sectaries, for example, had relatively little to say on the subject. The confession of faith issued by the Particular Baptists in 1644 did not even devote a separate article to the sacrament. Extreme sectaries, such as William Erbury and the Quakers, simply rejected it altogether, and emphasised instead the mystical communion of believers with Christ in the Spirit.[39]

Bunyan regarded the Lord's supper much as he did the sacrament of baptism. Those who partook of the sacrament were expected to possess the requisite "Light", and the sacrament was more important for its doctrinal significance than for its ceremonial aspect. The one significant difference between the two sacraments, Bunyan asserted, was that the Lord's supper, unlike baptism, was an ordinance "for the Church, as a Church. . . ." The individualistic nature of baptism was replaced by the societal character of the Lord's supper. The latter was described by the Bedford preacher as "a part of that Worship which Christ hath Instituted for his Church, to be Conversant in as a Church;

presenting them as such, with their Communion with their Head, and with one another as Members of him".[40]

The Lord's supper also differed from baptism with respect to the question of church membership. Although a man might become a member of a church without baptism because he lacked the necessary "Light", he could not continue membership in the church without being properly enlightened concerning the Lord's supper. The reason, explained Bunyan, was because the Lord's supper was part of the duty of the church *qua* church: "Wherefore this being a Duty incumbent on the Church, as a Church; and on every Member of that Body as such, they are obliged in that case more closely to deal with the Members, than in that wherein they are not So concerned; and with which as such, they have Nothing to do."[41] In all likelihood, therefore, the examination of a candidate for church membership included not only questions on his religious experience, but also questions and/or instruction concerning the proper nature of the Lord's supper. In any case, the Lord's supper was not a divisive issue within any particular group of sectaries.

The Christian Life

AS Water is that Element in which the Fish liveth; so Grace is that which is the life of the Saint.
As Gods grace is the salt of Saints, so Saints are the salt of God. The one is tne salt of God in the heart, and the other is the salt of God in the world.[42]

The life of the Christian pilgrim, whose earthly sanctuary was the ecclesiastical palace, revolved, in Bunyan's eyes, wholly around the grace of God. By the continual communication of divine grace into their souls believers were enabled to progress on their pilgrimage. "The Child by nature nuzels [*sic*] in its Mother's Bosom for the Breast; the Child by Grace, does by Grace seek to live by the Grace of God." Apart from the continual supply of this grace from its divine source it was, according to Bunyan, impossible for the elect "to do and suffer, and to manage our selves in doing and suffering according to the will of God". In order to live this Christian life there had to be infused into the justified sinner "a Root, a Principle of Grace with its continual supplies for the perfecting of that Salvation that God has designed for us". The continual supplies of this grace were likened by Bunyan to "*Aqua-vitae*" because they consistently quickened and revived the weary pilgrim on his taxing journey.[43]

Grace was not, however, a panacea which provided a heavenly bliss for the pilgrim's trek. Bunyan acknowledged that grace brought knowledge and strength, but he also cautioned that "the more Grace, . . . the greater Trials". Those who were recipients of grace were expected to live fruitful and productive lives, for grace "can no sooner appear to the soul, but it causeth this blessed fruit in the heart and life. . . ." The prominent recurring theme in *Christian Behaviour* was the unwavering proclamation that justification *sola gratia* and *sola fide* did not mean a life of irresponsibility; rather such justification necessitated the perpetual doing of good works. Hence there was a definite sense of activism which characterised the Christian life. That activism was based essentially on the bestowal of divine grace to the believer and the latter's use of that grace:

> Those Christians that are most laborious for God in this World, they have already most of him in their Souls, and that not onely because diligence in Gods wayes, is the meanes whereby God communicates himself; but also because thereby the senses are made more strong, and able, by reason of use to understand God, and to discern both good and evill.

Greater grace meant, therefore, not only greater trials but also greater activity. Such an attitude was fairly common among Protestants, especially Calvinist preachers. That attitude was reflected in an observation of Thomas Goodwin's which Bunyan would have found agreeable: Goodwin called the attention of his readers to the "difference of *Lux* and *Lumen*, Light and Shining of that Light", and suggested that *lux* was the grace which filled the hearts of saints whereas *lumen* was the good works "for which that Light is ordained. . . ."[44]

The responsibility incumbent on a recipient of grace was defined by Bunyan in terms of required duty or service. The greater the service required of a pilgrim, the greater the amount of grace bestowed upon him. "Thou desirest abundance of Grace; thou doest well, and thou shalt have what shall qualifie and fit thee for the service, that God has for thee to do for him. . . ." The supply of grace given to any individual, in other words, was directly related to the assistance he required for the fulfilment of his duty. Thus, for Bunyan grace was an energising principle bestowed by God upon his elect to enable them to fulfil their predetermined tasks. Such a concept of grace was common to Calvinist writers. John Owen, for example, defined grace as "that Influence of power whereby the Saints are enabled to performe particular Duties according to the mind of God. . . ." Bunyan would have fully agreed.[45]

Virtually every Calvinist preacher found himself trapped between the predestinarian logic of his theology and the practical exigencies of preaching to a struggling congregation. Clearly such preachers were aware that even the most saintly of the elect were not always faithful in performing the duties of the Christian life. Bunyan certainly realised this. Although he averred that divine grace and Christian obligations were "ties and binding things", he also felt compelled to warn his readers that "men of great Grace may grow consumptive in Grace, and idleness may turn him that wears a Plush Jacket, into Rags".[46] Consequently it was up to the pilgrim effectively to make use of that grace in the service for which it was intended to assist.

Grace specifically gave the believer certain "graces" or works of the Spirit at the time of his conversion. These graces, according to Bunyan, accompanied justifying righteousness, and were a *sine qua non* of the Christian life since "natures ability depends upon Graces. . . ." Because of the imperfections of the human nature and the opposition of the earthly man, however, none of these graces "can do their Work in us without shortness. . . ."

None of the graces could ever be perfected in a saint, according to Bunyan, yet all could be strengthened through faith. Yet because of their interdependence, the weakening of one grace meant the weakening of all: "As vices hang together, & have the links of a chain, dependance one upon another, even so the graces of the spirit also, are the fruits of one another, and have such dependance on each other, that the one cannot be without the other." A very similar statement was made by Thomas Goodwin, who wrote: "Graces, they are all of a knot, break one, and all fall asunder. . . ."[47]

The number of graces enumerated by Bunyan were manifold. The "root" grace Bunyan indicated to be faith, the quintessence of Christian obedience. Another grace was love, which Bunyan rapturously depicted as the quintessence of all gospel graces. Other graces were hope, patience, meekness, silence, long-suffering, and humility. Prayer and repentance were graces, as was filial fear, which Bunyan regarded as the highest duty of the believer to God. To be destitute of such fear was to be destitute of all other graces. Zeal, reverence, and meditation were additional graces, as were simplicity, sincerity, gentleness, self-denial, and a desire for righteousness. In short, Bunyan's list of graces provides a summary description of the characteristics regarded as essential for a good pilgrim.

In view of the importance of these graces for the Christian life it is not surprising to find Bunyan exhorting his readers to "get those graces now that will prove true graces then [i.e., at the final judgement], and therefore try them you have, and if upon tryall they prove not right, cast them away, and cry for better, lest they cast thee away, when better are not to be had. . . ." Baxter similarly exhorted his readers to "stir up then the Grace that is given you, and use Christs means, and do your best. . . ." The passivity of the sinner at conversion thus became radically transformed in the Christian life to the most fervent and intense activity—though this activity was never divorced by the Calvinist preacher from grace. Consequently, Bunyan urged the saints to "get more grace"; this they were to do by increasing their knowledge of Christ, praying, condemning their own sins, and subjecting themselves to the authority of the grace already reigning within them. What the pilgrim in the Christian life was never to forget was that "a good improvement of what we have of the grace of God at present, pleases God, and ingages him to give us more: but an ill improvement of what we at present have, will not do so". Therefore, "get more grace". The seeming illogicality of a Calvinist minister urging his congregation to "get more grace" was the distinctive irony of the general Puritan-sectarian tradition. The passivity inherent in the logic of a predestinarian philosophy was replaced by a fervent activism rooted in the psychological needs of proving oneself a member of the elect.[48]

NOTES

1. XXVIII, pp. 49–51.
2. LIX, Vol. II, 104–105; XXXVI, pp. 108, 157; IV, p. 31.
3. XX, p. 26; X, p. 8; XLV, p. 10; Dent, *Path-Way,* p. 409.
4. Nuttall, *Visible Saints: The Congregational Way* 1640–1660 (Oxford, 1957).
5. *The Church Book of Bunyan Meeting* 1650–1821, ed. G. B. Harrison (1928), pp. 1C–2. Cf. Nuttall, *Visible Saints,* pp. 44–50; noting especially the parallel examples of the churches at Broadmead, Bristol, and Bury St. Edmunds, Suffolk.
6. *Church Book,* pp. 50–51; XLV, p. 40; XX, p. 147.
7. XXVIII, pp. 50–51; *Church Book,* p. 17 (cf. the case of Brother Smith of Kempston, recorded on this page, for an example of this principle in practice).
8. *Church Book,* p. 2; *The Confession of Faith, of Those Churches which Are Commonly (though Falsly) Called Anabaptists* (1644), art. xxxiii; LVII, Vol. II, 56.
9. *Church Book,* p. 1C; LVII, Vol. II, 61 (italics mine); *Reliquiae Baxterianae,* Appendix III, p. 62.
10. *Church Book,* p. 2; IX, p. 12 (see Nuttall, *Visible Saints,* pp. 119–20, for a list of other churches following the same practice); LVII, Vol. II, 59, 61; Baxter, *Plain Scripture Proof;* LVII, Vol. II, 59.
11. XXXVI, p. 115; *Church Book,* pp. 54, 66, 53, 54; XXXVI, p. 149. The Particular Baptist *Confession* (1644), art, xlii, states: "Christ has . . . given power to his whole Church to receive in and cast out, by way of Excommunication, any member; and this power is given to every particular Congregation, and not [to] one particular person, either member or Officer, but the whole."

12. *Westminster Confession,* XXX, ii–iv; X, p. 49; Bayly, *Pietie,* p. 393.
13. LVII, Vol. II, 62; Baxter, *Church Concord* (1691; pt. 1 was, according to the title page, actually written in 1655), pt. 1, p. 15; and *The English Nonconformity* (1689), p. 150; Ussher, *Body of Divinitie,* p. 396; Nuttall, *Visible Saints,* p. 134 (cf. pp. 132–34).
14. XX, pp. 239–40; LVII, Vol. II, 70 (cf. pp. 56–58); XX, pp. 243–44, 241.
15. XXXVI, p. 65; LVII, Vol. II, 61; IV, p. 9.
16. XXVIII, pp. 2–3.
17. XXXVI, p. 40; Baxter, *Treatise of Conversion,* p. 233; XLIII, pp. 400–401.
18. *Church Book,* pp. 50–51; XXXVI, pp. 7, 91; XX, pp. 72, 82; X, p. 19.
19. VI, p. 41; XX, pp. 246–47.
20. XXXVI, p. 7; *Church Book,* p. 51 (italics mine); XX, pp. 206, 75–76, 182; Baxter, *Directions for Weak Distempered Christians* (1669), pt. 1, p. 130.
21. III, p. 17; LVII, Vol. II, 59; IX, pp. 41, 71.
22. LVII, Vol. II, 59; XLV, p. 24; LVII, Vol. II, 59 (cf. p. 61).
23. XLIV, p. 242; XLIII, p. 389 (cf. Bayly, *Pietie,* p. 677); XX, p. 184.
24. Bayly, *Pietie,* p. 510; Baxter, *Catholick Theologie,* Bk. I, pt. 2, chaps. lx, lxviii–lxxi; and Bk. I, pt. 3, p. 14; *Plain Scripture Proof,* pp. 113, 224—25, 327; Kiffin, *A Sober Discourse* (1681), fols. A3 verso-A4.
25. IX, p. 50 (cf. pp. 13, 17); D[anvers], "A Postscript" to *Treatise of Baptism* (1673), p. 51; T. Paul, *Some Serious Reflections* (1673), pp. 50–51; IX, pp. 81, 50.
26. LVII, Vol. II, 60, 61; Danvers, "A Postscript" to *Treatise of Baptism,* pp. 52, 44; Baxter, *A Christian Directory* (1673), pt. 3, pp. 805–806.
27. Danvers, *Treatise of Baptism,* pp. 27–28 (cf. T. Paul, *Some Serious Reflections,* p. 52); IX, p. 84; LVII, Vol. II, 62; Powell, *Christ and Moses,* pp. 50–52; Saltmarsh, *The Smoke in the Temple* (3rd ed.; 1646), p. 9.
28. LIX, Vol. II, 103 (cf. p. 109); LVII, Vol. II, 64; Denne, *Truth Outweighing Error,* pp. 90–91.
29. LVII, Vol. II, 66–67; T. Paul, *Some Serious Reflections,* p. 29; IX, p. 57; Kiffin, *Sober Discourse,* p. 161.
30. LVII, Vol. II, 63, 66; *Church Book,* p. 3; Fox, *Journal* (1911 ed.)' I, 254; Denne, *Truth Outweighing Error,* p. 60.

31. LVII, Vol. II, 65, 68; Danvers, "A Postscript" to *Treatise of Baptism*, pp. 52–53 (cf. Denne, *Truth Outweighing Error*, pp. 52–58); LVII, Vol. II, 65; Denne, *Truth Outweighing Error*, pp. 97–98; Baxter, *Christian Directory*, pt. 2, p. 806.

32. LVII, Vol. II, 65; T. Paul, *Some Serious Reflections*, p. 7; IX, p. 17; Denne, *Truth Outweighing Error*, pp. 78–79, 73.

33. LVII, Vol. II, 64; T. Paul, *Some Serious Reflections*, p. 8; IX, p. 19; LVII, Vol. II, 64.

34. LVII, Vol. II, 64; T. Paul, *Some Serious Reflections*, pp. 18–19, 16; IX, p. 34.

35. Saltmarsh, *Sparkles of Glory*, pp. 82–83. Cf. *Smoke in the Temple*, p. 12; William Dell, *Baptismon Didache: or, the Doctrine of Baptismes* (1648), p. 11; William Erbury, *The Testimony of William Erbery* (1658), pp. 55, 303; Fox, *Journal* (1911 ed.), II, 129; and *Gospel-Truth Demonstrated*, ed. George Whitehead, *et al.* (1706), p. 24; Barclay, *Apology*, pp. 290, 293ff. Cf. Nuttall, *The Holy Spirit*, pp. 99–101.

36. Baxter, *Treatise of Conversion*, p. 174.

37. IX, p. 91; LVII, Vol. II, 60; Baxter, *Weak Christians*, pt. 1, p. 84; LVII, Vol. II, 63; IX, pp. 58, 54.

38. LVII, Vol. II, 61, 64; XLVIII, p. 81; Baxter, *Plain Scripture Proof*, p. 329; XXI, fol. A7.

39. Erbury, *Testimony*, pp. 55, 303; Fox, *Journal* (1911 ed.), I, 253–54, 325; and *Gospel-Truth Demonstrated*, p. 24; Barclay, *Apology*, pp. 317ff. Cf. Nuttall, *The Holy Spirit*, pp. 98–101.

40. IX, pp. 18, 32, 51–52; VI, p. 33.

41. IX, p. 18. Cf. Kiffin, *Sober Discourse*, p. 10.

42. XLI, pp. 24–25; XXI, p. 179.

43. LIV, pp. 272, 287, 288 (cf. Owen, *Of Communion* [Oxford, 1657], p. 229); XX, p. 252; XXVIII, p. 43.

44. XLIV, p. 254; LVI, p. 573; XXXIV, p. 72; T. Goodwin, *Works*, V, pt. 2, p. 89.

45. XLIV, p. 253; Owen, *Of Communion*, p. 232.

46. XXXVI, p. 35; XLIV, p. 254.

47. LIII, p. 409; XLIII, p. 378; XXXIX, p. 101; T. Goodwin, *Works*, II, pt. 4, p. 277.

48. XXXVIII, p. 40; Baxter, *Weak Christians*, pt. 1, p. 158; XXI, pp. 189, 190. Cf. Owen, *A Complete Collection of the Sermons of . . . John Owen, D.D.*, ed. John Nesbitt, *et al.* (1721), p. 525.

6 Conclusion

CRITICS AND HISTORIANS of Bunyan have generally referred to him as a Calvinist and have done little to evaluate either his doctrine or the extent to which his doctrine was influenced by previous and contemporary theological thought. From the outset it must be admitted that it is impossible to analyse Bunyan's theology into compact and precisely defined sections and to attribute each of them to some particular source of influence. Like most writers Bunyan assimilated what he read and what he was taught, so that in the end what he expressed in his writings was a unique blending of existing ideas coloured and transformed in various ways by his own convictions, study, and experience. Throughout his writings it is, nevertheless, possible to indicate at various points distinctive ideas and tendencies gleaned from Luther, Calvinism, Antinomianism, and the founding principles of the Bedford church.

The fallacious tendency of most of Bunyan's critics and historians to speak of him simply as a Calvinist was noted by Henri Talon when he observed that "Luther's strong influence . . . is only touched on and not given its due prominence by Bunyan's critics. . . ."[1] Talon, however, failed equally to explain the extent of Luther's influence on Bunyan's thought. At the opposite extreme from those who refer to Bunyan as a representative of the Calvinism of the Puritan period[2] is S. T. Coleridge, who observed that "Bunyan may have been one [i.e., a Calvinist], but I have met with nothing in his writings (except his Anti-paedobaptism, to which too he assigns no saving importance) that is not much more characteristically Lutheran. . . ."[3] Neither extreme is correct.

Bunyan himself said little about those who influenced him, but was instead more inclined to regard the source of his work as wholly biblical:

> I have not writ at a venture, nor borrowed my Doctrine from libraries. I depend upon the sayings of no man: I found it [referring in this instance to the theme and substance of *Light for Them That Sit in Darkness*] in the Scriptures of Truth, among the true sayings of God.

When Fowler appealed, in his treatise on *The Design of Christianity*, to the Continental reformers Calvin, Peter Martyr, Wolfgang Musculus, and Jerome Zanchy, Bunyan simply replied: "It matters nothing to me, I have neither made my Creed out of them, nor other, then the Holy Scriptures of God." In the course of a later debate he informed his opponents: "Expositors I reverence, but must live by mine own Faith. . . ." He might just as well have said, "by mine own interpretation of the Bible", for his faith was never divorced from the fundamental principle, "I call for Scripture".[4]

The biblical passages to which Bunyan referred most frequently, as did his contemporaries, were those of the Pauline writings. In concluding his attack against Fowler, for example, Bunyan quoted ten verses from the Bible: six from the Pauline writings, one from Hebrews (which was then generally though not universally considered to be a work of Paul), two from the Johannine writings, and one from I Peter. There were several reasons for this attraction, not the least of which was the similarity of the experiences of conversion shared by Paul and Bunyan. It was Luther's commentary on Paul's Epistle to the Galatians which so profoundly influenced Bunyan. Paul was a favourite of the Calvinists as well, for it was from his writings that they gleaned, among other things, the scriptural basis for their doctrine of predestination. Finally, one of the paramount themes in Paul's epistles was the doctrine of grace, and it was only natural that

Bunyan should have been drawn to these epistles both as an expression of a man of like conviction and experience, and as a source of material for the development of his own doctrinal thought, the focal point of which was grace. "Paul was", in Bunyan's judgement, "one of the Pipes thorow which God conveyed this Grace to the World. . . ." Bunyan's constant admiration was apparent for this "man of men, who had so much Grace, revelation of grace, and Communion with Christ, that sometimes he knew not whether he was in or out of the body. . . ."[5]

Bunyan's reverential testimony concerning Luther's commentary on Galatians has already been recorded,[6] and it remains only to summarise the extent to which this work influenced his doctrine of grace. When Christian was making his tortured journey through the valley of the shadow of death (cf. Psalm xxiii. 4), "he thought he heard the voice of a man, as going before him . . .",[7] a man who may be identified not only as the Psalmist but as Luther also. Bunyan's conversion was markedly similar to that of Luther, as well as to those of Paul and Augustine, and because of their parallel experience Bunyan was more susceptible to Luther's influence than was someone who read him in a more objective sense and primarily as a theologian rather than as a spiritual "voice . . . as going before. . . ." Arising directly out of their experiences of conversion the influence of Luther on Bunyan's concept of the nature of God can be seen especially in Bunyan's view of God fundamentally in terms of the wrath-grace dichotomy rather than in terms of the Calvinist emphasis on the sovereign will of God. The controlling motif in Bunyan's theology was not the more philosophical principle of the divine will exercising supreme control in the universe, but the more personal and experiential conflict which raged in both the convicted sinner and the converted pilgrim who sensed on the one hand the dread of a God whose wrath could not be mitigated because of the wrong done to his holiness and justice, and on the other hand the all-sufficient grace of a God whose love and mercy had triumphed in the salvation of his elect.

Because of the intense reality of the wrath-grace dichotomy in their personal conversion as well as in their general concept of the nature of God, soteriology was of prime importance for both Luther and Bunyan. It was God as saviour rather than as ruler that was foremost in their minds—a God who would provide a means of salvation from the ghastly punishment to be meted out upon man by the divine wrath. Salvation in this sense, then, was for Bunyan as it was for Luther a present possession rather than a process. Such salvation centred, in Luther's thought, around the focal point of justification, a justification which was *sola gratia* and *sola fide*—totally devoid of the necessity of works. Luther's repeated emphasis of this theme in his commentary on Galatians left an indelible impression on Bunyan, who was adamant in the complete repudiation of the necessity of works for justification. For Bunyan it was, in essence, a matter of justification by the law or justification by grace, and when stated in this manner there was, if one wanted to adhere as closely as possible to the Pauline message, only one acceptable choice. It was upon this law-grace motif that Bunyan built—in the tradition of seventeenth-century Calvinists—his system of the covenants.

It is evident, therefore, that Luther exercised appreciable influence on Bunyan in the closely related areas of the nature of God, the basic concept of salvation *per se*, the necessity of justification *sola gratia* and *sola fide*, and the unalterable opposition of the law and grace. There were other points of similarity, such as their mutual recognition of the word of God as the primary means of grace and their concept of the Christian life as a life of grace and freedom, but these do not display the definite stamp of Luther's influence as do the concepts already noted.

On this Lutheran foundation Bunyan built an essentially Calvinist superstructure with the ideas which he assimilated from the writings of Bayly and Dent, the teaching of Gifford and Burton, his ministerial association with men such as Owen, and his contact in general with the recurrent and often controversial discussion of basic Christian principles which absorbed the minds of so many in the seventeenth century. His concept of the nature of God was quite compatible with the doctrine of the atonement which he learned from orthodox Calvinism, and the Anselmic satisfaction theory regarded as the norm by orthodox Calvinists was clearly expressed in his writings. Similarly, he limited the extent of grace in the atonement to the elect, but unlike Owen he was not bitterly opposed to those who asserted a general atonement. The influence of contemporary Calvinism on Bunyan, however, was most striking in his detailed exposition of the covenants. This point alone is sufficient to disprove Coleridge's assertion that Bunyan was a Lutheran, for Luther was in no sense a covenant theologian. It has been clearly demonstrated that Bunyan's development of the covenant scheme was fundamentally in accord with that of contemporary strict Calvinists, though it is also true to say that his tendency to Antinomianism in this regard stemmed from his Lutheran concept of the absolute polarity of law and grace.

Bunyan was also indebted to Calvinism for his concept of salvation as a process and not merely a present possession. Salvation began with the election and reprobation (or non-election) of mankind, and Bunyan's statement of this doctrine was wholly Calvinist, with one exception. In the *Westminster Confession* and the writings of Owen, to use two obvious examples, predestination was a doctrine derived from the prior principles of the absolute sovereignty of the divine will and the concomitant decrees pronounced by that will, whereas in the writings of Bunyan the doctrine of predestination originated primarily in a soteriological concern, with men being predestined more on the basis of foreknowledge and gracious love than as the result of abstract philosophical principles. In order that predestination be accomplished there had to be the effectual and irresistible calling of those predestined to glory, and in stating this doctrine Bunyan continued to draw upon his Calvinist mentors and associates. The remainder of his soteriology manifested consistent if not especially noteworthy Calvinist influence.

Bunyan's debt to Calvinism was by and large a debt to strict rather than to moderate Calvinism. The tendency of the latter to elevate the importance of such things as the Mosaic law and sanctification (at the expense, in Bunyan's eyes, of justification by faith) or to assert the possibility—if not the actuality—of atonement without satisfaction, was wholly unacceptable to

Bunyan. His tendency was rather to lean towards Antinomianism, though the extreme subjectivity characteristic of some Anti-nomians was equally unacceptable to him. Antinomian influence on Bunyan's thought is apparent at several places, notably in his emphasis on the covenant between the Father and the Son in which the elect were represented, in his eventual adoption of the Antinomian position that the elect were justified prior to faith and before creation, and in his insistence on the newness of the law in the covenant of grace and sanctification.

Influence of yet another sort was exerted upon Bunyan by the ecclesiastical tradition of which he was a part. On the basis of existing evidence it is reasonable to conclude that his ecclesiology was almost wholly a heritage from Gifford and Burton and the Bedford elders. There are striking similarities in phraseology between the enunciation of Bunyan's position on church com-munion and the prior principles established in that regard by the Bedford church, as recorded in the *Church Book*. The decision of the founding members of the congregation not to require baptism for membership was accepted—and eloquently defended—by Bunyan. His writings also included the four basic ecclesiological principles of the Independent-Baptist tradition, namely, separa-tion, fellowship, freedom, and holiness. It was not this tradition as a whole which influenced him, however, for he repudiated on the one hand the baptismal covenant and on the other the necessity of baptism for church membership. It was the teaching of the Bedford church which he adopted on this matter, and as the result of his position he attributed no real significance to the sacraments, especially baptism. By regarding them as the "shadowish, or figurative Ordinances" Bunyan moved in the direction of the Quakers' outright rejection of them. Of this he was not unaware, and thus declared that "I . . . dare not remove them, as some do, from the place, and end, where by God they are set and appointed. . . ."[8]

If the Quakers can be said to have exercised any influence on Bunyan it was virtually wholly in a negative capacity. Against their tendency to spiritualise Bunyan reacted by asserting an almost crass objectivity based on an infallible Bible and fortified by the tenets of scholastic Calvinism. The extent to which Bunyan would have resorted to Calvinist dogma in formulating his theology, had he not felt the need for such dogma as ammunition in his crusade against the Quakers, perhaps is debatable. When the Quakers had become an established force in religion and the militant crusading spirt of the fiery convert that he was had mellowed, Bunyan did not hesitate to assert that men must have "Light" before they submit themselves to baptism. If total reliance on the Inner Light in matters of the Christian faith was objectionable, it was equally wrong, according to Bunyan, to rely wholly upon external standards apart from the inner conviction brought about by the Holy Spirit.

No single theological label without careful qualification will fit Bunyan. He was bitterly opposed both to Arminianism and to Quakerism, and he was neither a moderate Calvinist nor a true Antinomian, although at certain points his doctrine was harmonious with Antinomian tenets. His foundation principles were basically Lutheran, but much of his theology was in full accord with the orthodox Calvinism of his period. His doctrine of the church and sacraments was neither Calvinist nor Lutheran but a heritage from the Independent-Baptist tradition, particularly the segment of that tradition of which he was a part.

Bunyan's thought as a whole was based on the doctrine of the grace of God revealed in Christ—a concept which permeated the whole of his writings and which was the focal point of his preaching and thinking. Because grace was its dominating motif, his thought retained a personal element which was often lacking in the writings of many Calvinists, notably those of Owen and the *Westminster Confession*. This sense of personal contact and vibrancy was, however, perhaps due more to the style of his writing than to his concern with grace; yet the concept of grace must be considered an important contributing factor to this personal element which pervaded his writings, since grace *per se* lent itself to a more personal treatment than did, for example, the more abstract concepts of sovereignty and will which were the basic principles of contemporary Calvinist theology.[9] It was precisely this personal and living quality which made his sermons and writings so

JOHN BUNYAN

popular, for through the spoken and the printed word he made the workings of divine grace come alive, so that not only he but his hearers and readers were contemporary with such works of grace as the making of the covenant between the Father and the Son, election, and the victory of Christ in the atonement.

It was this success in making what might have been nothing more than an abstract doctrine a living reality which must be regarded as the outstanding achievement of Bunyan as far as his thought is concerned. The fetters of scholastic Calvinism could not bind the resurgent consciousness of the work of grace within, nor could the harshness of Calvinist predestinarian dogma conquer the inner spring of emotion and love which urged all sinners to accept the offer of grace. There was at first the compulsion to preach "what I felt, what I smartingly did feel . . . ."[10] Then the pilgrim matured—"Christiana's route is the same as her husband's, but where for him darkness brooded, for her there is light"[11]—but always there remained that motivating force of transforming grace which neither maturity nor theological awareness diminished. This, coupled with his skill "in the direct colloquial expression of truth,"[12] was the key to the success which he achieved as a writer and a preacher.

NOTES

1. Talon, *John Bunyan,* p. 272.
2. Cf., e.g., Maurice Hussey, "The Humanism of John Bunyan," *From Donne to Marvell,* ed. Boris Ford (Penguin ed., 1956), pp. 219–31.
3. *The Literary Remains of Samuel Taylor Coleridge,* ed. H. N. Coleridge (1836–39), III, 398.
4. XXVI, fol. A4; VIII, p. 29 (cf. Fowler, *Design,* p. 84); IX, p. 30; LIX, Vol. II, 109.
5. VIII, p. 112; XLI, p. 95; XXI, p. 71. T. Goodwin praised Paul as "the highest example of grace, but Christ that ever was upon the Earth. . . ." *Works,* I, pt. 1, p. 233. Cf. Grantham, *Christianismus Primitivus,* Bk. II, p. 48.
6. See the Introduction.
7. XXVIII, p. 80.
8. LVII, Vol. II, 59.

9. Cf. O. E. Winslow's observation that "Bunyan has taken religion out of the realm of confused mystery, made it personal, and given it a relation to life as it is lived in a practical world." *John Bunyan*, p. 210. Cf. also R. M. Frye, *God, Man, and Satan: Patterns of Christian Thought and Life in Paradise Lost, Pilgrim's Progress, and the Great Theologians* (Princeton, New Jersey, 1960), p. 410.

10. XVI, sect. 229.

11. Talon, *John Bunyan* ("Writers and Their Work Series"; 1956), p. 27.

12. Hussey, *From Donne to Marvell*, p. 219.

Glossary

Antinomianism
The term derives from the Greek words *anti*, "against," and *nomos*, "law." It properly refers to those who asserted that the Mosaic law was abrogated for Christians living under the covenant of grace. The ramifications of the Antinomian position are discussed in Chapter Four.

Arminianism
A school of theological thought named after the Dutch professor Jacobus Arminius (1560–1609). Its five principal tenets are: (1) God predestined to save those who believed and persevered, but he did not predetermine who they would be; (2) Christ died for all men, though the benefits of his death were restricted to believers only; (3) man is dependent on divine grace to attain saving faith; (4) grace is not irresistible; (5) perseverance is dependent on grace, but is not absolutely certain. Essentially, Arminians emphasised the role of human choice and responsibility in religion, though never without recognising the necessity of divine grace.

Calvinism
As it is used in this study, Calvinism refers to the broad school of theological thought which accepted the following tenets: (1) God predestined certain specific individuals to salvation, with the remainder being left without hope; (2) Christ died for the

elect alone; (3) mankind is totally depraved; (4) the effectual working of grace cannot be resisted; (5) the elect will persevere to the end, and cannot fall from the state of grace. Calvinism embraced varying shades of opinion, but essentially Calvinists emphasised the sovereignty of God and the inability of depraved man to act apart from the effectual working of grace. English Calvinists in the seventeenth century fell basically into two categories: strict and moderate, as explained in Chapter Four. For a discussion of the relationship between Calvin's own theology and the development of that theology subsequently, see *John Calvin,* ed. G. E. Duffield (Appleford, Berkshire, 1966; *Courtenay Studies in Reformation Theology,* I), chaps. 1 and 2.

Diggers
A movement peculiar to Puritan England which embraced sectarian religious views, opposition to monarchic government, and a fervent belief in a communistic society. Its leader, the mystic Gerrard Winstanley, in company with a small group of followers attempted unsuccessfully to launch his communal society at St. George's Hill, Surrey, in 1649.

Election
The decision by God to grant certain men eternal life. For the Calvinist, election was an arbitrary choice of God; for an Arminian, election was based on an individual's faith.

Enthusiasm
Belief in divine inspiration or possession by the Holy Spirit, customarily in the absence of external means.

Eschatology
The branch of theology which deals with "the last things," i.e. death and resurrection, the final judgement, heaven and hell, etc.

Fifth Monarchy Men
A politico-religious movement in Puritan and Restoration England which attracted a variety of sectaries and miscellaneous

radicals. They believed in the imminent return of Christ to establish the world's last and fifth monarchy (the others being the Babylonian, Persian, Greek, and Roman). Their immediate task was generally conceived to be the forceful seizure of the state and the establishment of a government of saints.

Imputation
The attribution of something to another person, especially the attribution of the righteousness of Christ to believers. The various interpretations of imputation in the context of the doctrine of justification are discussed in Chapter Three.

Infralapsarianism
The term derives from the Latin words *infra*, "later than," and *lapsus*, "the fall." It is the theological belief that God permitted the fall of man rather than ordaining it, and that he based predestination on his knowledge that men would be in a sinful state by their own choice. Supralapsarians, on the other hand, believed that God predestined men, and then decreed the fall in order to enact his plan.

Justification
The divine act of pronouncing or making a sinner righteous in the sight of God, or of forgiving him because of the atonement of Christ. The exact meaning of justification was hotly disputed. The varying interpretations are discussed in Chapter Three.

Levellers
A political movement in Puritan England led by John Lilburne (d. 1657) which attracted numerous sectaries. The Levellers advocated a major extension of the franchise (but not to the extent of universal suffrage), religious toleration, and the reordering of society.

Omnipotence
The theological concept that the power of God is without limitation.

Omniscience
The theological concept that the knowledge of God is all-encompassing and without limitation.

Paedobaptists
Those Christians who practised the baptism of infants.

Predestination
The theological doctrine that God preordained men either to salvation or to damnation, the former through the act of election, and the latter through the act of reprobation. The varying concepts of predestination are discussed in Chapter Two.

Reprobation
In Calvinism, either the positive decree of God to relegate certain men to eternal damnation, or the decision of God to leave certain men without effectual means to obtain salvation. See Chapter Two.

Sanctification
The life-long process of making a Christian holy, of changing the entirety of his being to bring it into conformity with the moral and ethical principles of Christianity. See Chapter Three.

Socinianism
A religious movement spearheaded by the Italians Lelio and Fausto Sozzini in the sixteenth century, largely in Poland. The movement spread to Holland and England as well as other places. Socinians rejected the doctrine of the Trinity, the theological tenets of Calvinism, and the satisfaction theory of the atonement.

Sola Fide
By faith alone, not by faith and works.

Sola Gratia
By grace alone—an act of divine love and mercy. In Protestant thought, salvation viewed from the divine perspective is *sola gratia*, whereas viewed from the human perspective it is *sola fide*.

Soteriology
The doctrine of salvation in Christian theology, which embraces such subordinate doctrines as predestination, calling, justification, and sanctification. Chapters Two and Three discuss the many aspects of soteriology in Puritan and sectarian thought.

Bibliography of Bunyan's Works

[Place of publication is London. Roman numerals refer to the works of Bunyan as cited in the footnotes.]

    I. *The Acceptable Sacrifice.* 1689.

   II. *The Barren Fig-Tree.* 1688.

  III. *A Book for Boys and Girls.* 1686.

  IV. *A Case of Conscience Resolved.* 1683.

   V. *A Caution to Stir up to Watch against Sin.* [1684].

  VI. *Christian Behaviour.* 1663.

 VII. *Come, & Welcome, to Jesus Christ.* 1678.

VIII. *A Defence of the Doctrine of Iustification, by Faith.* 1672.

  IX. *Differences in Judgment about Water-Baptism, No Bar to Communion.* 1673.

   X. *A Discourse of . . . the House of God.* 1688.

  XI. *A Discourse upon the Pharisee and the Publicane.* 1685.

 XII. *The Doctrine of the Law and Grace Unfolded.* 1659.

XIII. *Ebal and Gerizzim, ad cal. One Thing is Needful.* 3rd ed., 1688.

XIV. *A Few Sighs from Hell.* 1658.

 XV. *Good News for the Vilest of Men.* 1688.

XVI. *Grace Abounding to the Chief of Sinners.* 1666.

XVII. *Idem* 6th (enlarged) ed., 1688.

XVIII. *The Greatness of the Soul.* 1683.

XIX. *The Heavenly Foot-Man.* 1698.

XX. *The Holy City.* 1665.
XXI. *A Holy Life.* 1684.
XXII. *The Holy War.* 1682.
XXIII. *Instruction for the Ignorant.* 1675.
XXIV. *I will Pray with the Spirit.* 2nd ed., 1663.
XXV. *The Life and Death of Mr. Badman.* 1680.
XXVI. *Light for Them That Sit in Darkness.* 1674.
XXVII. *One Thing Is Needful.* 3rd ed., 1688.
XXVIII. *The Pilgrim's Progress.* 1678.
XXIX. *Idem* 2nd ed., 1678.
XXX. *Idem* The Second Part. 1684.
XXXI. *Prison-Meditations, ad cal. One Thing Is Needful.* 3rd ed., 1688.
XXXII. *Profitable Meditations.* [1661].
XXXIII. *Questions about . . . the Seventh-Day-Sabbath.* 1685.
XXXIV. *The Resurrection of the Dead.* [c. 1665].
XXXV. *Seasonable Counsel.* 1684.
XXXVI. *Solomon's Temple Spiritualiz'd.* 1688.
XXXVII. *Some Gospel-Truths Opened according to the Scriptures.* 1656.
XXXVIII. *The Strait Gate.* 1676.
XXXIX. *A Treatise of the Fear of God.* 1679.
XL. *A Vindication of . . . Some Gospel-Truths Opened.* 1657.
XLI. *The Water of Life.* 1688.
XLII. *The Work of Jesus Christ as an Advocate.* 1688.

The following works were published by Charles Doe for the first time in *The Works of That Eminent Servant of Christ, Mr. John Bunyan,* 1692.

XLIII. *Christ a Complete Saviour.*
XLIV. *The Desire of the Righteous Granted.*
XLV. *An Exposition on the First Ten Chapters of Genesis.*
XLVI. *Israel's Hope Encouraged.*
XLVII. *Of Antichrist and His Ruine.*
XLVIII. *Of Justification by an Imputed Righteousness.*

XLIX. *Of the House of the Forest of Lebanon.*
    L. *Of the Law and a Christian.*
   LI. *Of the Trinity and a Christian.*
  LII. *Paul's Departure and Crown.*
 LIII. *The Saints Knowledge of Christ's Love.*
 LIV. *The Saints Privilege and Profit.*
  LV. *A Mapp Shewing the Order & Causes of Salvation and Damnation.* (Reprinted in the 1692 edition of Bunyan's works from a copy which is now lost or destroyed.)
 LVI. *Saved by Grace.* (Reprinted in the 1692 edition of Bunyan's works from a copy which is now lost or destroyed.)

The following works were reprinted for the first time in an expanded edition of the 1692 edition of Bunyan's works. This edition was edited by John Wilson and published in 1736–37.

 LVII. *A Confession of My Faith.*
LVIII. *Mr. Bunyan's Last Sermon.*
 LIX. *Peaceable Principles and True.*

Selected Secondary Sources on Bunyan

Brown, John. *John Bunyan* (1628–1688): *His Life, Times, and Work.* Tercentenary ed., revised by F. M. Harrison, London, 1928. The standard reference for Bunyan's life.

Frye, R. M. *God, Man, and Satan: Patterns of Christian Thought and Life in Paradise Lost, Pilgrim's Progress, and the Great Theologians,* Princeton, New Jersey, 1960. A provocative study in comparative literature, concentrating on the literary expression of theology.

Fullerton, W. Y. *The Legacy of Bunyan,* London, 1928. A popular treatment of Bunyan's life and thought by a modern devotee.

Griffith, G. O. *John Bunyan,* London, 1927.

Harrison, F. M. *A Bibliography of the Works of John Bunyan,* Oxford, 1932. A convenient reference work. *John Bunyan, A Story of his Life,* London, 1928, and reprinted 1964. One of the better Tercentenary biographies marking the anniversary of Bunyan's birth.

Harrison, G. B. *John Bunyan: A Study in Personality,* London, 1928.

Hussey, Maurice. "The Humanism of John Bunyan," *From Donne to Marvell,* ed. Boris Ford, London, Penguin Paperback, 1956. A scholarly discussion of a neglected side of Bunyan's writing.

JOHN BUNYAN

Kaufmann, U. M. *The Pilgrim's Progress and Traditions in Puritan Meditation*, New Haven, Conn., 1966.

An excellent recent study of the literary methods employed by Bunyan to convey his message. The bibliography contains references to prior studies of Bunyan's mode of writing.

Sharrock, Roger. *John Bunyan*, London, 1954.

A good biography by a foremost authority on Bunyan.

"Personal Vision & Puritan Tradition in Bunyan," *The Hibbert Journal*, LVI (October, 1957), 47–60.

An excellent study of the social and intellectual milieu in which Bunyan developed and worked.

Talon, Henri. *John Bunyan: The Man and His Works*, trans. Barbara Wall, London, 1951.

The best recent biography; written by a Frenchman.

Tindall, W. Y. *John Bunyan: Mechanick Preacher*, New York, 1934.

An indispensable study of the uneducated lay preachers of the mid-seventeenth century, and the role played by Bunyan in their movement.

Winslow, O. E. *John Bunyan*, New York, 1961.

A recent and readable biography.

Index of Proper Names